Physics Education for Students: An Interdisciplinary Approach

Edited by

Maria Teresa Caccamo

&

Salvatore Magazù

Dipartimento di Scienze Matematiche e Informatiche
Scienze Fisiche e Scienze della Terra
Università di Messina
Messina
Italy

Physics Education for Students: An Interdisciplinary Approach

Editors: Maria Teresa Caccamo and Salvatore Magazù

ISBN (Online): 978-981-4998-51-2

ISBN (Print): 978-981-4998-52-9

ISBN (Paperback): 978-981-4998-53-6

© 2021, Bentham Books imprint.

Published by Bentham Science Publishers Pte. Ltd. Singapore. All Rights Reserved.

BENTHAM SCIENCE PUBLISHERS LTD.
End User License Agreement (for non-institutional, personal use)

This is an agreement between you and Bentham Science Publishers Ltd. Please read this License Agreement carefully before using the book/echapter/ejournal (**"Work"**). Your use of the Work constitutes your agreement to the terms and conditions set forth in this License Agreement. If you do not agree to these terms and conditions then you should not use the Work.

Bentham Science Publishers agrees to grant you a non-exclusive, non-transferable limited license to use the Work subject to and in accordance with the following terms and conditions. This License Agreement is for non-library, personal use only. For a library / institutional / multi user license in respect of the Work, please contact: permission@benthamscience.net.

Usage Rules:

1. All rights reserved: The Work is the subject of copyright and Bentham Science Publishers either owns the Work (and the copyright in it) or is licensed to distribute the Work. You shall not copy, reproduce, modify, remove, delete, augment, add to, publish, transmit, sell, resell, create derivative works from, or in any way exploit the Work or make the Work available for others to do any of the same, in any form or by any means, in whole or in part, in each case without the prior written permission of Bentham Science Publishers, unless stated otherwise in this License Agreement.
2. You may download a copy of the Work on one occasion to one personal computer (including tablet, laptop, desktop, or other such devices). You may make one back-up copy of the Work to avoid losing it.
3. The unauthorised use or distribution of copyrighted or other proprietary content is illegal and could subject you to liability for substantial money damages. You will be liable for any damage resulting from your misuse of the Work or any violation of this License Agreement, including any infringement by you of copyrights or proprietary rights.

Disclaimer:

Bentham Science Publishers does not guarantee that the information in the Work is error-free, or warrant that it will meet your requirements or that access to the Work will be uninterrupted or error-free. The Work is provided "as is" without warranty of any kind, either express or implied or statutory, including, without limitation, implied warranties of merchantability and fitness for a particular purpose. The entire risk as to the results and performance of the Work is assumed by you. No responsibility is assumed by Bentham Science Publishers, its staff, editors and/or authors for any injury and/or damage to persons or property as a matter of products liability, negligence or otherwise, or from any use or operation of any methods, products instruction, advertisements or ideas contained in the Work.

Limitation of Liability:

In no event will Bentham Science Publishers, its staff, editors and/or authors, be liable for any damages, including, without limitation, special, incidental and/or consequential damages and/or damages for lost data and/or profits arising out of (whether directly or indirectly) the use or inability to use the Work. The entire liability of Bentham Science Publishers shall be limited to the amount actually paid by you for the Work.

General:

1. Any dispute or claim arising out of or in connection with this License Agreement or the Work (including non-contractual disputes or claims) will be governed by and construed in accordance with the laws of Singapore. Each party agrees that the courts of the state of Singapore shall have exclusive jurisdiction to settle any dispute or claim arising out of or in connection with this License Agreement or the Work (including non-contractual disputes or claims).
2. Your rights under this License Agreement will automatically terminate without notice and without the

need for a court order if at any point you breach any terms of this License Agreement. In no event will any delay or failure by Bentham Science Publishers in enforcing your compliance with this License Agreement constitute a waiver of any of its rights.
3. You acknowledge that you have read this License Agreement, and agree to be bound by its terms and conditions. To the extent that any other terms and conditions presented on any website of Bentham Science Publishers conflict with, or are inconsistent with, the terms and conditions set out in this License Agreement, you acknowledge that the terms and conditions set out in this License Agreement shall prevail.

Bentham Science Publishers Pte. Ltd.
80 Robinson Road #02-00
Singapore 068898
Singapore
Email: subscriptions@benthamscience.net

CONTENTS

PREFACE i

LIST OF CONTRIBUTORS iii

CHAPTER 1 EXPANSIVE FRAMING PRODUCES MORE VIVID INTRODUCTORY PHYSICS LABS 1
Danny J. Doucette and *Chandralekha Singh*
- INTRODUCTION 1
- PHYSICS LABS 3
- BIOMEDICAL APPLICATIONS 5
- NATURE OF SCIENCE 7
- CONCLUSION 9
- CONSENT FOR PUBLICATION 9
- CONFLICT OF INTEREST 9
- ACKNOWLEDGEMENTS 9
- REFERENCES 10

CHAPTER 2 ACTIVE LEARNING IN STUDYING PHYSICS AS THE FIRST RESEARCH EXPERIENCE OF UNIVERSITY STUDENTS 13
Elena Kazakova, Svetlana Kirpu, Marina Kruchek, Elena Moshkina, Olga Sergeeva and *Elena Tikhomirova*
- INTRODUCTION 14
- ORGANIZATION OF PROJECT ACTIVITIES IN PHYSICS 16
    - Involving Students in Performing a Demonstration Experiment in Physics ... 16
    - Students' Preparation for Seminar Presentations on the Topics that Require Physical Demonstrations 17
    - Students' Development of Working Models of Devices that Demonstrate Physical Phenomena and Processes 17
    - Students' Research on Physical Topics 19
- ORGANIZATION OF INTERDISCIPLINARY PROJECT WORK 20
- CONCLUSION 22
- CONSENT FOR PUBLICATION 22
- CONFLICT OF INTEREST 22
- ACKNOWLEDGEMENTS 22
- REFERENCES 22

CHAPTER 3 CAN PHYSICS EDUCATION SUPPORT A SELF-RESPONSIBLE SOCIETY? 24
Gilbert Ahamer
- INTRODUCTION 24
- PHYSICS LABS FIRST DIDACTIC METHOD "3×7 = 21" 25
    - Didactic Basics of the Course Design "3×7 = 21" 25
    - Considering Several Value Systems Means An Inter-Paradigmatic Approach ... 25
    - The Concrete Didactic Process of "3 x 7 = 21" 26
    - Reflection of the "3 x 7 = 21" Process 29
    - Web Design for "3 x 7 = 21" 33
- SECOND DIDACTIC METHOD: THE JET PRINCIPLE IN E-LEARNING ... 33
    - Introduction and Motivation for the "Jet Principle" 33
    - Understanding the Design of the "Jet Principle" 34
    - Inventing a "Jet Engine" for Smoothing Learning Processes 35
    - Symbolic Interpretation of the Analogy with a Jet Engine 36

  The "Jet Principle" in (E-)Learning 37
  Description of the "Jet Principle" Process 39
  Summary of the "Jet Principle" Process 42
  Web Design for the "Jet Principle" in E-Learning 43
 CONCLUSIONS 44
 CONSENT FOR PUBLICATION 44
 CONFLICT OF INTEREST 44
 ACKNOWLEDGEMENTS 44
 REFERENCES 44

CHAPTER 4 DIALOGIC BEST PRACTICE FOR DISSEMINATION OF A SCIENTIFIC CULTURE 49
 Gilbert Ahamer
 SURFING GLOBAL CHANGE 49
  Pedagogic Foundation of the Negotiation Game "Surfing Global Change" 49
  Interdisciplinarity 54
  A Variety of Value Systems: Becoming Interparadigmatic 54
 THE RULES FOR THE GAME "SURFING GLOBAL CHANGE" 55
 OVERVIEW OF THE GAME "SURFING GLOBAL CHANGE" 64
 BASICS OF WEB DESIGN FOR SGC 66
 CONCLUSIONS 68
 CONSENT FOR PUBLICATION 69
 CONFLICT OF INTEREST 69
 ACKNOWLEDGEMENTS 69
 REFERENCES 69

CHAPTER 5 RESEARCH-BASED PROPOSALS ON OPTICAL SPECTROSCOPY IN SECONDARY SCHOOL 72
 Daniele Buongiorno and *Marisa Michelini*
 INTRODUCTION 72
 THE RESEARCH PERSPECTIVE 73
 THE GENERAL STRUCTURE OF THE EDUCATIONAL PATH 74
 CONTEXT, SAMPLE AND METHODOLOGY 77
 DATA ANALYSIS 79
  Masterclass(c) Experimentation: Post-test 80
  Summer School Experimentation: Pre- and Post-Test 82
 CONCLUSIONS 83
 CONSENT FOR PUBLICATION 84
 CONFLICT OF INTEREST 84
 ACKNOWLEDGEMENTS 84
 REFERENCES 84

CHAPTER 6 NORMAL MODE INVESTIGATION OF A SYSTEM OF COUPLED OSCILLATORS: A PHYSICS LECTURE 87
 Maria Teresa Caccamo and *Salvatore Magazù*
 INTRODUCTION 87
 THEORETICAL BACKGROUND 89
 EXPERIMENTAL SET-UP 96
 EXPERIMENTAL PROCEDURE 97
  Experimental Data 98
  Data Analysis 99
 HISTORICAL BACKGROUND: FOURIER AND WAVELET TRANSFORMS 101

APPLICATION OF FOURIER AND WAVELET TRANSFORMS	106
CONCLUDING REMARKS	107
CONSENT FOR PUBLICATION	108
CONFLICT OF INTEREST	108
ACKNOWLEDGEMENTS	108
REFERENCES	108

SUBJECT INDEX 113

PREFACE

The Special Issue titled *Physics Education for Young Students* is mainly addressed to new approaches and trends in teaching and learning specific topics of Physics to young university students. It is well known that, from a general point of view, Physics teaching and learning cover, with different extents, several fields, such as for example Laboratory activities, Mathematics, Philosophy and History. These distinguished areas can generate complexities and difficulties for students in learning some concepts since the same topics are often presented following approaches that do not highlight the existing correlations among the involved disciplines. Therefore, in order to enrich topics with high value meanings, it is important to propose and to promote integrated and interdisciplinary approaches where Laboratory activities in a wide sense, pose themselves as fundamental tools to improve the knowledge of some topics which interest different aspects of Physics, Mathematics, Philosophy and History.

In fact, it is well known that, especially in a teaching context, interdisciplinarity consists in "bringing together at least two disciplines, in order to develop an original representation of a notion, a situation, a problem" [1]. An interdisciplinary approach can provide a solution to many student comprehension problems and can bring a deeper understanding and appreciation: the more the students learn, the more they find common basis for all the interested disciplines; in other words, they learn more and improve their basis to tackle all disciplines. Furthermore, interdisciplinarity promotes the development of higher cognitive skills such as critical thinking, spirit of synthesis and integration, reflexive skills, understanding of difficult concepts and conceptual memory [2-4].

In this framework, the main aim of the proposed special issue is to promote Laboratory activities and Mathematics contents for Physics courses addressed to young university students, as well as to put into evidence the importance of an historical and philosophical approach which is a recurring topic nowadays due to the fact that scientific activity constitutes by itself a historical and a philosophical process.

In this framework the papers collected in this special issue are addressed to the understanding of the best practices involved in some specific topics teaching through an interdisciplinary approach, which requires the employment of different and complementary methodologies.

More in details, the issue is divided in 6 chapters.

In chapter 1, the authors explore the design and implementation of laboratory courses starting from the analysis of student's interviews and coursework considered as the best practice for the implementation of introductory Physics laboratory courses when seeking to adopt an interdisciplinary approach [5].

In chapter 2, the authors highlight the concept of active learning as first research experience of university students. For this purpose they believe that the development of students' research skills should be carried out both within the class hours and within out-of-class studies through complementary activities. Furthermore, they believe that such tasks make it possible to expand the scope of students' active-learning activities, to broad students' scientific horizons, and to form the skills of a researcher [6].

The author of chapters 3 and 4 raises the question about which educational and didactic strategies, based on self-responsibility, are the most suitable for spreading a humanitarian culture based on science. To answer this question, at first, the author proposes two didactic approaches for strengthening self-responsibility in students: the approach called "3 x 7 = 21" and the approach called "jet principle"; then, in chapter 4, the author explains the five-level structure of rules and provides a few results on resulting social dynamics in student groups. All the considered approaches rely on the dialogue and the confrontation of learners with their peers and are suitable for advanced physics students in any transdisciplinary setting [7-8].

The authors of chapter 5 present a proposal for a lecture on optical spectroscopy as dealt in a secondary school. In particular, they designed an educational path for secondary school students encompassing experimental approaches while, from the theoretical point of view, they designed intervention modules in which interpretative issues are problematized using Inquiry-Based Learning strategies [9].

Finally, in chapter 6, the authors present a lecture addressed to first year Physics students on a system of coupled oscillators. In particular, they point out how in order to improve the understanding of this Physics topic, it is important to integrate theory with experiments. For this reason, they first describe the dynamics of the system from a theoretical point of view, then describe the experiment execution and finally analyze the results by comparing the Fourier transform and the Wavelet transform approaches[10].

REFERENCES

[1]   G. Fourez, and A. Maingain, A. and B. Dufour, *Approches didactiques de l'interdisciplinarité.*, DeBoeck Université: Bruxelles, 2002.

[2]   L. Erickson, *Designing Integrated Curriculum that Promotes Higher Level Thinking.* Association for Supervision and Curriculum Development: Alexandria, VA, 1996.

[3]   J.T. Klein, "L'éducation primaire, secondaire et postsecondaire aux États-Unis: vers l'unification du discours sur l'interdisciplinarité", *Rev. Sci. Edu.*, vol. XXIV, no. 1, pp. 51-74, 1998.

[4]   W. Spady, *Outcome-based education: Critical issues and answers.* American Association of School Administrators: Arlington, VA, 1994.

[5]   D. Doucette, and C. Singh, "Expansive Framing Produces More Vivid Introductory Physics Labs", *Physics Education for Young Students: An Interdisciplinary Approach,* Bentham Science, 2020.

[6]   E. Kazakova, S. Kirpu, M. Kruchek, E. Moshkina, O. Sergeeva, and E. Tikhomirova, "Active Learning as The First Research Experience of University Students", *Physics Education for Young Students: An Interdisciplinary Approach,* Bentham Science, 2020.

[7]   G. Ahamer, "Can physics education support a self-responsible society?", *Physics Education for Young Students: An Interdisciplinary Approach,* Bentham Science, 2020.

[8]   G. Ahamer, "Dialogic best practice for dissemination of a scientific culture", *Physics Education for Young Students: An Interdisciplinary Approach,* Bentham Science, 2020.

[9]   D. Buongiorno, and M. Michelini, "Research-based proposals on optical spectroscopy in secondary school", *Physics Education for Young Students: An Interdisciplinary Approach,* Bentham Science, 2020.

[10] M. T. Caccamo, and S. Magazù, "Normal Mode Investigation of a System of Coupled Oscillators: a Physics Lecture", *Physics Education for Young Students: An Interdisciplinary Approach,* Bentham Science, 2020.

Maria Teresa Caccamo
&
Salvatore Magazù
Dipartimento di Scienze Matematiche e Informatiche
Scienze Fisiche e Scienze della Terra
Università di Messina
Messina
Italy

List of Contributors

Chandralekha Singh	Department of Physics and Astronomy, University of Pittsburgh, Pittsburgh, Pennsylvania 15260, USA
Daniele Buongiorno	URDF (Unità di Ricerca in Didattica della Fisica) - Università degli Studi di Udine, Italy
Danny J. Doucette	Department of Physics and Astronomy, University of Pittsburgh, Pittsburgh, Pennsylvania 15260, USA
Elena Moshkina	Institute of Physics and Technology, Petrozavodsk State University, Petrozavodsk, Russian Federation
Elena Kazakova	Institute of Physics and Technology, Petrozavodsk State University, Petrozavodsk, Russian Federation
Elena Tikhomirova	Institute of Foreign Languages, Petrozavodsk State University, Petrozavodsk, Russian Federation
Gilbert Ahamer	Karl-Franzens University Graz, Institute for Economic and Social History, Universitätsstrasse 15/F2, 8010 Graz, Austria
Marina Kruchek	Institute of Mathematics and Information Technologies, Petrozavodsk State University, Petrozavodsk, Russian Federation
Marisa Michelini	URDF (Unità di Ricerca in Didattica della Fisica) - Università degli Studi di Udine, Italy
Maria Teresa Caccamo	Dipartimento di Scienze Matematiche e Informatiche, Scienze Fisiche e Scienze della Terra, Università di Messina, Italy
Olga Sergeeva	Institute of Physics and Technology, Petrozavodsk State University, Petrozavodsk, Russian Federation
Svetlana Kirpu	Institute of Foreign Languages, Petrozavodsk State University, Petrozavodsk, Russian Federation
Salvatore Magazù	Dipartimento di Scienze Matematiche e Informatiche, Scienze Fisiche e Scienze della Terra, Università di Messina, Italy

CHAPTER 1

Expansive Framing Produces More Vivid Introductory Physics Labs

Danny J. Doucette[1,*] and **Chandralekha Singh**[1]

[1] Department of Physics and Astronomy, University of Pittsburgh, Pittsburgh, Pennsylvania 15260, USA

Abstract: Expansive framing, which positions students as participants in larger conversations that span time, place, people and disciplines, can be a valuable approach for designing curricula and learning experiences, to help students learn physics through an interdisciplinary approach. This chapter reports on the efforts to use expansive framing as a guiding principle while transforming and revitalizing an introductory physics laboratory class. This chapter, describes student experiences with two central elements of the lab course that are strongly influenced by the concept of expansive framing and related to interdisciplinary learning. First, we sought to incorporate and emphasize experiences related to the students' real-world and professional experiences, such as connections between biology and physics, that will be interesting for the health-science majors who take the lab. Second, we sought to promote discussions between students and their graduate student instructors about the epistemology of experimental physics, which we refer to as the nature of science, which is an important interdisciplinary goal for the lab class. We explore the need, design, and implementation of these two elements of the lab course by analyzing student interviews and coursework. Consequently, we propose that using expansive framing for the design of student learning should be considered a best practice for implementing introductory college physics laboratory courses when seeking to adopt an interdisciplinary approach to student learning.

Keywords: Expansive framing, Nature of science, Physics education.

INTRODUCTION

What does it mean to learn something? One answer involves the concept of transfer, or the ability to take the knowledge learned in one context and applying it in a different context [1]. Based on the goal of improving transfer, expansive framing is an approach to curriculum and learning activity design that focuses on the need to situate learning and learning contexts within the broader scope of learners' settings, roles, disciplines, and experiences [2].

---

[*] **Corresponding author Danny J. Doucette:** Department of Physics and Astronomy, University of Pittsburgh, Pittsburgh, Pennsylvania 15260, USA; Tel/Fax: 412-624-9000; E-mail: danny.doucette@pitt.edu

Maria Teresa Caccamo and Salvatore Magazù (Eds.)
All rights reserved-© 2021 Bentham Science Publishers

To understand expansive framing, it may be useful to start off with its antithesis, bounded framing. Learning activities that employ bounded framing presume that the concepts students learn are relevant only for limited contexts. These limited contexts might include specific places, times, and participants. For example, physics learners might perceive that Newton's laws of motion apply to physics problems, but are not relevant in the physical world, in their other classes, or in their future studies or career. Such a perception might develop if student learning concentrates on solving problems set in artificial contexts, regardless of the instructor's intentions or their own perspective that the laws of physics are general and broadly applicable. Bounded framing may also limit the intellectual role played by students, situating them at the periphery of the learning process [3, 4].

By contrast, expansive framing promotes students' understanding of concepts by connecting different contexts, developing links between settings and roles to create intercontextuality [5]. Intercontextuality empowers learners to make connections and transfer knowledge between different learning contexts (including time, location, and participants), roles, and topics. Intercontextuality supports transfer by helping learners connect learning context to the transfer context by way of the encompassing context. In this view, if student learning is supported with expansive framing then students may begin to make connections between the content, the learning context, and the encompassing context. Later on, when students are asked to transfer their understandings, the intercontextuality makes it easier for them to connect ideas from the learning context and encompassing context with the transfer context [2].

In an experiment with high school biology students, Engle, Nguyen, and Mendelson found that students who were tutored with an expansive framing demonstrated substantially better transfer of their learning to a new context [5]. In this experiment, students were provided with tutoring about the cardiovascular system on day one, and then asked to transfer their understanding to the respiratory system on the other day. Students received the same tutoring, but different kinds of framing. Students in the control group experienced tutoring that was framed in a typical way, while students in the experimental condition experienced tutoring with expansive framing that focused on context, topic, and roles. When interacting with students in the experimental condition, the tutors provided an expansive framing to the context of tutoring by describing the experiment as a multi-day study (rather than two separate days), located at the university (rather than contained in the specific room), and conducted with a team (rather than with just one tutor). The tutors also described the topic of the study as "body systems" (rather than the cardiovascular and respiratory systems separately) and they emphasized that the participants were authors responsible for their own ideas (rather than recipients of ideas from others). These modest changes to the framing of the learning scenario produced dramatically improved transfer from students [5]. Another study by Engle found that an expansive framing helped 5th grade students in a science lesson [6]. In this case, the two important aspects of expansive framing were temporal connections with other contexts and the roles of the learners as members of a larger community of people interested in the topic.

Related studies in physics education have analyzed the roles of framing and scaffolding [7] when students solve isomorphic problems [8 - 11], categorize problem types [12 - 15], and self-diagnose their answers to quizzes [16 - 18]. these studies' results serve to underline the difficulty of knowledge transfer for introductory physics' students while suggesting that both scaffolding and framing could play a valuable role in improving transfer [19 - 22].

Expansive framing can be a useful approach to interdisciplinary education. By bringing a focus to transfer and intercontextuality, expansive approaches to lesson and curriculum design encourage educators to think about how learners can make meaningful connections between the physics they learn in their classes and their personal interests and career goals [23]. Likewise, the nature of intercontextuality calls educators to ask increasingly fundamental questions about the learning goals of their courses, which may result in questions and issues that are broader than the scope of any one course, or even any one discipline.

In this chapter, we will outline how expansive framing was used in the design of student learning activities in an introductory physics lab course. First, we will consider how expansive framing was used to guide the development of lab-work. By seeking to make learning meaningful for students, many on health-science career tracks, we created opportunities for students to demonstrate transfer. This included both bringing ideas and skills from their other studies and interests into the physics lab, as well as applying physics concepts in the context of their other studies and interests. Second, we will examine how we used expansive framing to improve student learning about the nature of science during the lab course. As a fundamentally interdisciplinary topic, the nature of science is a good example of intercontextuality. This allowed for ample opportunity for students to reflect on elements of the nature of science in the context of the physics lab as well as in other contexts.

PHYSICS LABS

The introductory physics lab has long been a cornerstone in college education [24]. Traditional approaches to physics lab instruction rely on highly-structured experimental work [25, 26]. In this approach, students carefully follow instructions in a lab manual to conduct an experiment that has been designed for them. One aim of these highly-structured labs is to give students practice collecting and analyzing data to verify theoretical predictions. However, many students fail to see the larger goal, focusing instead on completing the assigned work step-by-step as quickly as possible, or as diligently as possible, to obtain their desired grades and leave. These students have adopted a bounded framing. They view their experimental work as something that is done in the lab, for a limited time, and for a limited purpose. They see their role in the lab as a procedure-follower rather than a knowledge-creator, and they are unlikely to make connections between the work they do in the lab and the physics concepts they study in class, other lab-work, or other disciplines of study.

One alternative approach to highly-structured introductory labs is skills-based labs. These labs omit the reinforcement of physics concepts as a goal, and instead focus on helping students develop their scientific thinking skills through experimental work [27 - 29]. The skills-based approach may allow for expansive framing, for example, if students are reminded that scientific thinking skills are useful in other scientific disciplines.

Another alternative to highly-structured introductory labs is conceptual labs. In conceptual labs, experimental work is deployed to help students learn and practice their understanding of physics concepts [30]. For example, students may develop hypotheses based on physics principles and then test their hypotheses immediately using simple, hands-on equipment. Concept-based labs may also be conducive to expansive framing, as they may allow connections to be made between lecture and the lab, between different labs, and even between the world of conceptual physics and the external world.

Our introductory lab is a one-semester, 2-credit course that is offered separately from the two-course sequence of introductory physics lectures. Students work in pairs (occasionally triplets, if there is an odd number), with up to 24 students per lab section. Each lab section is instructed by a graduate student teaching assistant (TA). Since health science majors are required to take the physics lab, but engineering students are not, the majority of the students who take the lab are interested in pursuing careers in the health sector. A smaller number are physical science majors. For both health science majors and physical science majors, the introductory physics lab may be the only (or the last) time these learners will encounter experimental physics. A few physics majors also take the lab, but they will take further lab courses in physics. For these students, the value of the lab is in how physics concepts and ways of thinking relate to the students' own studies, interests, and lives. Thus, we seek to include interdisciplinary learning in the lab learning activities and curriculum through the use of expansive framing.

BIOMEDICAL APPLICATIONS

Since many of the students in our introductory labs are pursuing health science careers, the traditional, highly structured, labs were designed to include biomedical applications where possible. Typically, students would conduct experiments using traditional physics apparatus and then, for the last section, apply the same physics concepts to a biological context. For example, after a lab on physical optics and lenses, students used a model of the human eye with a water-filled "lens" that could be expanded or contracted to see how accommodation works in human vision. Another example is using a blood pressure cuff to measure blood pressure when a human arm is held at different heights, as part of a lab about Bernoulli's Principle. Students also took measurements using an EKG as part of a lab about DC circuits, briefly examining the relationship between the length of their legs and their natural gait at the end of a lab about simple harmonic motion and pendula, and learned about the theory of colors by examining spectra using a diffraction spectrometer. These activities are described in [26]. Activities such as these have been shown to foster students' interest [31].

These elements of the lab work contain implicit expansive framing. The message they convey is that physics is applicable, and undergirds thephenomena from biomedical contexts, too. Students are encouraged to connect expertise from other disciplines with their studies in physics. This helps students appreciate the intercontextuality of the physics concepts from these labs, including the idea that lenses, pressure, electric currents, and simple harmonic motion are concepts that manifest in a variety of contexts.

In semi-structured interviews conducted at the end of the semester, we asked students to discuss the labs they remembered best or appreciated the most. These biomedical applications came up frequently in their responses. Ray, a neuroscience major planning to apply to medical school, described the model of the human eye as his favorite lab, saying, "we used the set-up of the eye to see where the light would focus for hyper and myopia. That was pretty cool." Zara, an anthropology major planning to apply to medical school, explained that she liked the eye model best because of the connection to a context of interest to her, explaining that "learning about the eye kind of overlaps with the anatomy that I'm interested in." Ray and Zara vividly remembered this lab experience because it connected to their interests, allowing them to develop an intercontextuality that included the concept of a lens in both physical and medical contexts.

Liza, another pre-med student, preferred the blood pressure lab activity. "I really liked when there was an application to healthcare-related things. So, like, the lab when we did the blood pressure, that was really cool." Mira, a biology major from a family of doctors, also liked the blood pressure lab, explaining that she had "never thought of how raising or lowering your arm could affect the blood pressure." Meanwhile, an economics major and pre-medical student Kamala described liking the EKG lab activity, saying, "I was really excited. PQRS waves. I know what valve was closing to, I knew the physiology behind it, so seeing an EKG was really exciting." Liza, Mira, and Kamala valued the biological applications because these applications allowed them to view their role as a learner expansively. They were able to connect contexts and leverage their interest and expertise in medical topics to gain deeper understanding of the activity they were doing in the physics lab.

However, just because a lab activity had an interdisciplinary connection to biology or medicine did not mean that the activity empowered students to frame their learning expansively. Expansive framing requires more than just an activity that is related to biomedical applications. For example, none of the students we interviewed remembered the activity in which they measured the length of their leg and period of their gait. In that activity, which aimed to help students see their legs as physical pendula while they walked, students were not provided any clues or connections as to how the activity was supposed to connect to their interests in medicine, the kinesiology of the human body, or their experiences in other science classes. Instead, it was perceived simply as a strange activity with no apparent relevance to their lives or interests.

On a similar note, Kamala, who liked the EKG activity, reported being frustrated by an activity involving color theory that came at the end of a lab in which students used a diffraction spectrometer. She saw no connection between the manipulation of light that she was doing on her lab bench and color formation by mixing light. Nor did the activity help her view the spectrometer lab expansively. Thus, it is important that lab activities seeking to provide students with opportunities to engage with physics concepts expansively be presented in a way that allows the students to make connections to pre-existing knowledge from another context, such as another class or an outside interest or expertise, or with another role, such as the students' self-concept as a pre-med student. Simply including ostensibly-relevant activities in the lab curriculum is not enough. Instead, as we saw in the case of the eye model, EKG, and blood pressure activities, the benefits of expansive framing can only be realized when learning activities include clear connections to the encompassing context, such as students' interests.

Finally, it is worth noting that expansive framing in introductory lab courses is not limited to connections with students' career plans. Janet, another pre-med student, described not a biomedical lab activity, but a simple practical lab activity when we asked her to describe her favorite lab experience. "I really enjoyed the first lab, the roller coaster. You have a thing, you drop a metal ball. Those are really fun because you see the effect of gravity on different weights of the ball. I think something that could be better is, instead of just testing two balls, what if we tested different materials? Like, how does the material affect the weight and all that stuff, and what could you predict as the distances, and stuff like that. That's something that's interesting." Her explanation of why she liked the standard ball-on-a-ramp lab demonstrates a kind of expansive framing that focuses on her curiosity and, ultimately, her role as an inquirer in the lab context. Expansive framing that situates students in the role of an investigator is eminently suited to the physics lab, including both the skills-based and conceptual labs described in the preceding section.

NATURE OF SCIENCE

We recently ascertained a need to do a better job of addressing the epistemology of experimental physics, sometimes called the nature of science [32], in our introductory labs. In part, this is a response to the AAPT Recommendations for the Undergraduate Physics Laboratory Curriculum [33]. We were also inspired by recent literature calling for introductory physics labs to help students learn critical and scientific thinking skills [28, 34]. The new nature of science dimension in our lab curriculum calls for students to learn about the significance and functioning of hypotheses, experimental design, correlational thinking, uncertainty, error, and the social dimension of scientific knowledge generation.

The nature of science is necessarily and unavoidably an interdisciplinary topic. Since it would be difficult to coordinate instruction about nature of science across disparate college departments, we are left to our own devices to figure out how to discuss this interdisciplinary topic in the physics lab. An expansive framing could provide the answer. An expansive framing elevates and recognizes students' expertise from other disciplines alongside their extracurricular interests. To help students learn the nature of science in the physics lab, then, we need to help students make explicit connections with their other courses and interests when we address nature of science questions. These connections, taken together, help to form an intercontextuality that both brings life to interdisciplinary essence of the nature of science while also helping students learn the topic by leveraging their expertise and interests from beyond the physics lab.

In our first attempt to introduce these concepts to the lab, we asked the graduate student teaching assistants (TAs) who taught the lab to take the lead. They were to reflect on their own understanding of the nature of science and then initiate conversations with students in the lab during 1-on-1 conversations each week as the topics arose organically through the lab work the students were performing. While the TAs initially showed interest, our observations and follow-up conversations indicated that the TAs did not initiate conversations about the nature of science in the lab, despite having opportunities to do so. They found it awkward to start such conversations when the students were focused on completing their lab work.

We may understand why this attempt was unsuccessful by considering the lack of an expansive framing lens in the design of this attempt. Because of its interdisciplinary essence, the nature of science inhabits a broader context than the lab work that students perform. We asked the TAs to invite students to engage in discussions in a context (*i.e.*, experimental science, broadly) that was significantly different from the narrow context of their lab work, but without providing any framing to encourage or support such discussions. In retrospect, we could see that the lab work the students performed was being understood with a bounded framing. The students thought of the experimental investigations as requiring skills and understandings that were only relevant within the narrow context of the physics lab, and adopted the limited role of experiment performer, following the instructions without pausing to think about larger issues.

Our second attempt was more successful. We re-wrote the lab curriculum to include explicit questions about the nature of science that students would answer during their lab work. One example question asked students to reflect on the role of predictions: "So far, in this lab report, you have made several different predictions. These predictions have been in the form of written text, graphs, and diagrams. Why are predictions so useful and important in experimental sciences like physics? Please write a paragraph response." We included one or two such questions each week, covering the breadth of the nature of science topics that were important for us, and including space for students to draw on their expertise from other disciplines and interests. In reviewing student lab reports, it is clear that students engaged deeply with these questions. Typical responses were reflective, thorough, and demonstrated a deep understanding of the topic.

Embedding nature of science questions in the lab work, along with explicit reinforcement from the TAs that these questions were valuable, served to expand the framing for the lab work to include the nature of science as an included topic for the physics lab. As the semester progressed, students began to demonstrate transfer from other contexts to the physics lab by using examples from other science labs, courses, and disciplines in their answers to the nature of science questions. For one nature of science question that asked students to reflect on the role of the terms "theory" and "law", and on the significance of named laws (like

"Snell's Law") in science, the majority of student responses included comparisons to the use of the terms "theory" and "law" in other scientific disciplines and the structural issue of the scientific establishment failing to adequately recognize the work of scientists from historically-marginalized groups, like Rosalind Franklin.

In parallel with the embedded nature of science questions, we also introduced a system of checkpoints in the lab work. When students reached a checkpoint, they called the TA over. The TA asked the students one or two open-ended questions, in order to prompt some broader thinking about scientific skills and concepts (including the nature of science). From an expansive framing point of view, these checkpoints served to reinforce both expansive contexts by asking questions that called students to consider the role of physics beyond the scope of the lab investigation they were conducting at that moment, in the physics lab. The checkpoints also served to provide an expansive framing to the role of the students in the lab. Instead of merely following the directions in the lab manual, the students were expected to take on the role of a thoughtful, reflective, knowledge generator.

CONCLUSION

As a tool for developing learning activities and introducing curricular transformations when interdisciplinary learning is a key priority, expansive framing may help student learners develop understandings that they are able to transfer to new contexts. Biomedical-related activities in our labs helped students frame physics concepts like blood pressure, lenses, and electric circuits in an expansive way. The framing empowered these students to transfer their knowledge both into and out of the physics lab. Likewise, when we used expansive framing to guide the introduction of explicit reflection about the nature of science into the lab course, students developed intercontextuality and were able to make thoughtful connections to other scientific disciplines. Thus, through expansive framing, students in our labs were able to engage with effective and meaningful opportunities to engage in interdisciplinary learning.

CONSENT FOR PUBLICATION

Not applicable.

CONFLICT OF INTEREST

The authors declare no conflict of interest, financial or otherwise.

ACKNOWLEDGEMENTS

Declared none.

REFERENCES

[1] D. L. Schwartz, J. D. Bransford, and D. Sears, "Efficiency and innovation in transfer", *Transfer of Learning from a Modern Multidisciplinary Perspective,* pp. 1-51, 2005.

[2] R.A. Engle, D.P. Lam, X.S. Meyer, and S.E. Nix, "How does expansive framing promote transfer? Several proposed explanations and a research agenda for investigating them", *Educ. Psychol.,* vol. 47, pp. 215-231, 2012.
[http://dx.doi.org/10.1080/00461520.2012.695678]

[3] R. J. Dufresne, T. Thaden-Koch, W. Gerace, and W. Leonard, "When transfer fails: Effect of knowledge, expectations and observations on transfer in physics", *Transfer of learning: Research and perspectives,* pp. 155-215, 2005.

[4] F. Reif, *Applying Cognitive Science to Education: Thinking and Learning in Scientific and Other Complex Domains* MIT Press: Cambridge, MA, 2008.

[5] R.A. Engle, P.D. Nguyen, and A. Mendelson, "The influence of framing on transfer: Initial evidence from a tutoring experiment", *Instr. Sci.,* vol. 39, pp. 603-628, 2011.
[http://dx.doi.org/10.1007/s11251-010-9145-2]

[6] R.A. Engle, "Framing interactions to foster generative learning: A situative explanation of transfer in a community of learners classroom", *J. Learn. Sci.,* vol. 15, pp. 451-498, 2006.
[http://dx.doi.org/10.1207/s15327809jls1504_2]

[7] A. Collins, J.S. Brown, and A. Holum, "Cognitive apprenticeship: Making thinking visible", *Am. Educ.,* vol. 15, pp. 6-11, 1991.

[8] C. Singh, "Assessing student expertise in introductory physics with isomorphic problems. I. Performance on nonintuitive problem pair from introductory physics", *Phys. Rev. Spec. Top-Ph,* vol. 4, p. 010104, 2008.
[http://dx.doi.org/10.1103/PhysRevSTPER.4.010104]

[9] C. Singh, "Assessing student expertise in introductory physics with isomorphic problems. II. Effect of some potential factors on problem solving and transfer", *Phys Rev Spec Top-Ph,* vol. 4, p. 010105, 2008.
[http://dx.doi.org/10.1103/PhysRevSTPER.4.010105]

[10] S.-Y. Lin, and C. Singh, "Using isomorphic problems to learn introductory physics", *Phys. Rev. Spec. Top-Ph,* vol. 7, p. 020104, 2011.
[http://dx.doi.org/10.1103/PhysRevSTPER.7.020104]

[11] S.-Y. Lin, and C. Singh, "Using an isomorphic problem pair to learn introductory physics: Transferring from a two-step problem to a three-step problem", *Phys. Rev. Spec. Top-Ph,* vol. 9, p. 020114, 2013.
[http://dx.doi.org/10.1103/PhysRevSTPER.9.020114]

[12] M. Chi, P.J. Feltovich, and R. Glaser, "Categorization and representation of physics problems by experts and novices", *Cogn. Sci.,* vol. 5, pp. 121-152, 1981.
[http://dx.doi.org/10.1207/s15516709cog0502_2]

[13] A. Mason, and C. Singh, "Assessing expertise in introductory physics using categorization task", *Phys. Rev. Spec. Top-Ph,* vol. 7, p. 020110, 2011.
[http://dx.doi.org/10.1103/PhysRevSTPER.7.020110]

[14] C. Singh, "Categorization of problems to assess and improve proficiency as teachers and learners", *Am. J. Phys.,* vol. 77, pp. 73-80, 2009.
[http://dx.doi.org/10.1119/1.2990668]

[15] A. Mason, and C. Singh, "Using categorization of problems as an instructional tool to help introductory students learn physics", *Phys. Educ.,* vol. 51, no. 025009, 2016.
[http://dx.doi.org/10.1088/0031-9120/51/2/025009]

[16] E. Yerushalmi, E. Cohen, A. Mason, and C. Singh, "What do students do when asked to diagnose their mistakes? Does it help them? I. An atypical quiz context", *Phys. Rev. Spec. Top-Ph,* vol. 8, p. 020109, 2012.
[http://dx.doi.org/10.1103/PhysRevSTPER.8.020109]

[17] E. Yerushalmi, E. Cohen, A. Mason, and C. Singh, "What do students do when asked to diagnose their mistakes? Does it help them? II. A more typical quiz context", *Phys. Rev. Spec. Top-Ph,* vol. 8, p. 020110, 2012.
[http://dx.doi.org/10.1103/PhysRevSTPER.8.020110]

[18] A. Mason, E. Yerushalmi, E. Cohen, and C. Singh, "Learning from mistakes: The effect of students' written self-diagnoses on subsequent problem solving", *Phys. Teach.,* vol. 54, pp. 87-90, 2016.
[http://dx.doi.org/10.1119/1.4940171]

[19] A. Maries, S.-Y. Lin, and C. Singh, "Challenges in designing appropriate scaffolding to improve students' representational consistency: The case of a Gauss's law problem", *Rev. Phys. Educ. Res,* vol. 13, p. 020103, 2017.
[http://dx.doi.org/10.1103/PhysRevPhysEducRes.13.020103]

[20] S-Y. Lin, and C. Singh, "Challenges in using analogies", *Phys. Teach.,* vol. 49, pp. 512-513, 2011.
[http://dx.doi.org/10.1119/1.3651738]

[21] S.-Y. Lin, and C. Singh, "Effect of scaffolding on helping introductory physics students solve quantitative problems involving strong alternative conceptions", *Phys. Rev. Spec. Top-Ph,* vol. 11, p. 020105, 2015.
[http://dx.doi.org/10.1103/PhysRevSTPER.11.020105]

[22] C. Singh, "Problem solving and learning", *AIP Conf. Proc.,* vol. 1140, pp. 183-197, 2009.
[http://dx.doi.org/10.1063/1.3183522]

[23] E.F. Redish, C. Bauer, K.L. Carleton, T.J. Cooke, M. Cooper, C.H. Crouch, B.W. Dreyfus, B.D. Geller, J. Giannini, J.S. Gouvea, M.W. Klymkowsky, W. Losert, K. Moore, J. Presson, V. Sawtelle, K.V. Thompson, C. Turpen, and R.K.P. Zia, "NEXUS/Physics: An interdisciplinary repurposing of physics for biologists", *Am. J. Phys.,* vol. 82, pp. 368-377, 2014.
[http://dx.doi.org/10.1119/1.4870386]

[24] G. DeBoer, *A History of Ideas in Science Education.* Teachers College Press, 2019.

[25] A.A. Bless, "Cook-book laboratory work", *Am. Phys. Teach.,* vol. 1, pp. 88-89, 1933.
[http://dx.doi.org/10.1119/1.1992836]

[26] R. Clark, *Introduction to Laboratory Physics.* 3rd ed. Kendall Hunt: Dubuque, IA, 2012.

[27] N. Holmes, *"Structured quantitative inquiry labs: Developing critical thinking in the introductory physics laboratory"*, Ph.D. thesis, University of British Columbia, Vancouver, BC, Canada, 2015.

[28] L. Bao, T. Cai, K. Koenig, K. Fang, J. Han, J. Wang, Q. Liu, L. Ding, L. Cui, Y. Luo, Y. Wang, L. Li, and N. Wu, "Physics. Learning and scientific reasoning", *Science,* vol. 323, no. 5914, pp. 586-587, 2009.
[http://dx.doi.org/10.1126/science.1167740] [PMID: 19179514]

[29] E. Etkina, and A. Van Heuvelen, "Investigative science learning environment–A science process approach to learning physics", *Research-Based Reform of University Physics,* pp. 1-48, 2007.

[30] D.R. Sokoloff, P.W. Laws, and R.K. Thornton, "RealTime Physics: Active learning labs transforming the introductory laboratory", *Eur. J. Phys.,* vol. 28, no. S83, 2007.
[http://dx.doi.org/10.1088/0143-0807/28/3/S08]

[31] B. D. Geller, C. Turpen, and C. H. Crouch, "Sources of student engagement in Introductory Physics for Life Sciences", *Phys. Rev. Phys. Educ. Res,* vol. 14, p. 010118, 2018.
[http://dx.doi.org/10.1103/PhysRevPhysEducRes.14.010118]

[32] N.G. Lederman, Nature of science: Past, present, and future.*Handbook of Research on Science*

Education, 2007, pp. 831-879.

[33] J. Kozminski, H.J. Lewandowski, N. Beverly, S. Lindaas, D. Deardorff, A. Reagan, R. Dietz, R. Tagg, M. Eblen-Zayas, J. Williams, and R. Hobbs, *AAPT Recommendations for the Undergraduate Physics Laboratory Curriculum.* American Association of Physics Teachers: College Park, MD, 2014.

[34] B. R. Wilcox, and H. J. Lewandowski, "Students' epistemologies about experimental physics: Validating the Colorado Learning Attitudes about Science Survey for experimental physics", *Phys. Rev. Phys. Educ. Res,* vol. 12, p. 010123, 2016.
[http://dx.doi.org/10.1103/PhysRevPhysEducRes.12.010123]

CHAPTER 2

Active Learning in Studying Physics as the First Research Experience of University Students

Elena Kazakova[1], Svetlana Kirpu[1], Marina Kruchek[1], Elena Moshkina[1], Olga Sergeeva[1] and Elena Tikhomirova[1,*]

[1] *Petrozavodsk State University, Russian Federation*

Abstract: Modern educational standards impose high requirements on the qualification of higher education graduates majoring in engineering and technical areas. The development of professional competencies is carried out both through students' educational activities and scientific research work. Research activities allow students to acquire the skills necessary to perform scientific research, develop independence and initiative, intensify students' cognitive activity, and contribute to creative thinking of a future engineer.

The authors of the article, being university lecturers in physics, mathematics, and English, share the experience of involving first-and second-year students of the Institute of Physics and Technology in research work through out-of-class activities. At the beginning of studies, students go through a period of adaptation to university environment; they have different levels of initial training and lack experimental skills. Nevertheless, during this period of study it is very important to give a student the opportunity to get a "feel" for science, so that a student has a chance to try and solve a task independently, even if it is not difficult enough, and, thus, to experience the joy of learning. Students' enthusiasm for learning should be taken into consideration as an important factor for the development of research skills. Teaching staff members need to take into account students' interests, give them the opportunity to develop their abilities, so that first- and second-year students could determine their own individual learning paths, despite the different levels of initial training in the subject and degrees of motivation. One way to solve this complicated problem is to involve students actively in learning.

Student's research work should be a comprehensive, goal-oriented and a methodically justified system, in which the complexity of the tasks being solved is consistently increasing. The authors believe that the development of students' research skills should be carried out both within the class hours and out-of-class studies through the following activities. In-class activities include performing mini-research projects, analyzing and processing results during laboratory work, preparing scientific reports for seminar presentations, involving students to perform a physics demonstration experiment in lectures. During extracurricular time, as part of out-of-class independent studies, stud-

---

[*] **Corresponding author Elena Tikhomirova:** Petrozavodsk State University, Russian Federation; Tel: +79212249570; E-mail: helenpetrova@list.ru

Maria Teresa Caccamo and Salvatore Magazù (Eds.)
All rights reserved-© 2021 Bentham Science Publishers

ents are encouraged to participate in a wide range of additional activities: conducting research for interdisciplinary projects, preparing a research report in a foreign lanuage as well, and creating working models of devices that demonstrate physical phenomena and processes. Such tasks make it possible to expand the scope of students' active-learning activities, broaden students' scientific horizons, and form the skills of a researcher.

As a result of ongoing work to involve first- and second-year students in research activities, the number of students participating in student scientific conferences and those awarded scholarships for successful participation in scientific research has increased. Student involvement in the educational process makes them an active part of it, enhances their personal capabilities, contributing to the formation of the required competencies, creating an atmosphere of development of scientific and creative potential, and laying the foundations for future research work in later years of study.

Keywords: Active learning, Foreign language, Individual learning paths, Interdisciplinary connections, Mathematics, Physics, Project-based learning, Students' research work.

INTRODUCTION

Modern educational standards impose high requirements on the qualification of higher education graduates majoring in engineering and technical areas. All over the world, there is a real need for professionally competent, socially active and competitive specialists who are ready to effectively conduct engineering activities at an interdisciplinary level, master advanced technologies in a short time, and are able to predict the consequences of their activities. Engineers are required not only to know a particular subject area but also to possess a system of fundamental and professional knowledge and skills to solve complex technical and technological problems. This means that the training of such specialists requires optimization of the university educational process, which includes the introduction of new educational methods (technologies) designed to develop both professional and general cultural competencies. One of the ways to improve the educational process, according to the authors, is the development of active learning methods aimed at acquiring research skills, self-organization and self-education skills, intensifying students' cognitive activity, and contributing to creative thinking of a future engineer.

It should be noted that the foundation of engineering education is, first of all, the proper level of mathematical apparatus, knowledge and understanding of the basic laws of physics, which are practically implemented in modern technology. Mathematics is a specific general education discipline since the knowledge obtained in mathematics is the foundation for studying other general education and special disciplines. On the other hand, mathematics is not a major subject for most areas of university training, and students, especially first- and second-year undergraduates, perceive it as a kind of abstract science. To change this situation, it is necessary to constantly show the connection of mathematics with problem-solving in the chosen field of study, since first- and second-year students do not yet have sufficient knowledge of special subjects and are not able to assess the value of knowledge and application of mathematical methods to solve these problems [1, 2].

In addition to sciences, due attention should be paid to humanities, one of which is a foreign language.

Thus, the training of engineering specialists requires a comprehensive approach to integrate physics with other disciplines taught to first- and second-year students. The article considers the experience of implementing an interdisciplinary approach in teaching physics, mathematics, and a foreign language.

Over the past few decades, an increasing number of educators and researchers in the field of education have noted in their works that students have difficulty learning physics [1, 3]. This is due to the falling interest in the exact sciences in general (including physics) and engineering disciplines. In many countries, the proportion of young people choosing these subjects is declining. As a result, applicants have insufficient training in physics and mathematics. When planning measures to improve the educational process and introduce new educational methods, it is necessary to take this fact into account. first of all, don't follow towards increasing the complexity or the amount of educational material, but towards increasing students' engagement in active learning and involvement in the knowledge attainment process.

These circumstances prompted the authors to search for active methods of teaching physics that ensure the intensive development of cognitive motivation and interest, and contribute to the expression of creative abilities in learning.

According to the authors, one of the promising directions in the development of active learning is students' involvement in research activities, starting from the first year. At the beginning of studies, students go through a period of adaptation to the university environment; they have different levels of initial training and lack experimental skills. Nevertheless, during this period of study it is very important to give a student the opportunity to get a "feel" for science, so that a student had a chance to try to solve a task independently, even if it is not difficult enough, and, thus, to experience the joy of learning. Students' enthusiasm for learning should be taken into consideration as an important factor for the development of research skills. Teaching staff members need to take into account students' interests, give them the opportunity to develop their abilities. Therefore, starting from the first days of students' being at university, lecturers try to identify those first-year students interested in modeling, programming and possess the skills to create their own appliances and devices, *etc.* [3, 4].

ORGANIZATION OF PROJECT ACTIVITIES IN PHYSICS

Students' project activities relate to problem-based learning and are regarded as one of developmental person-centered learning methods. Project activities are aimed at the development of independent research skills (problem statement, collection and processing of information, conducting experiments, and analyzing the results) and allow students to understand and apply the knowledge and skills acquired in the study of various disciplines. As a basis for these activities, we propose to use the STEAM model of education, wherein training is supposed to be built upon problem-oriented educational activities (project-based learning and engineering design), which combine scientific principles, technology, design, and mathematics into one STEAM program, implemented as a part of students' out-of-class studies under the guidance of teaching staff members as project supervisors [5, 6].

Students' research work should be a comprehensive, goal-oriented and methodically justified system, in which the complexity of the tasks being solved is consistently increasing. The development of students' research skills can be carried out in several directions. Students are invited to participate in various tasks that differ in both complexity and labor input: creating working models of devices that demonstrate physical phenomena and processes and so on; preparing scientific reports for seminar presentations, in a foreign language as well; conducting research for interdisciplinary projects. Such tasks make it possible to expand the scope of students' active-learning activities, broaden students' scientific horizons, and form the skills of a researcher [7 - 9]. Let us consider these areas of work in more detail.

Involving Students in Performing a Demonstration Experiment in Physics

To prepare and conduct a demonstration experiment in physics, students are given lectures on such topics as "The law of conservation of momentum", "The phenomenon of electromagnetic induction", "The law of conservation of mechanical energy", "The critical state of matter", "Fire piston", and others. Students prepare in advance to demonstrate experiments under the guidance of a lecturer. As a rule, the performance of these experiments does not require students to have the extra capabilities of the experimenter, but it introduces the necessary interactive component in the learning process, awakens interest in the topic, boosts student's self-esteem and contributes to the development of the required competencies. It turned out to be a successful experience to involve yesterday's applicants in speaking to schoolchildren: students presented and explained demonstration experiments in physics they had previously prepared.

Students' Preparation for Seminar Presentations on the Topics that Require Physical Demonstrations

The topics that the lecturer does not address in lectures are offered for presentations. In this regard, the topics that contain the material at the intersection of several parts of physics will be particularly valuable. The study of such material allows students to establish logical connections between concepts and phenomena, and develop cognitive abilities. Let us consider an example of a class on the topic "Liquid properties." During the class, students report about the phenomenon of surface tension, energy and force interpretation of the surface tension coefficient, surface active agents, wetting and non-wetting of a solid body with liquid, and capillary phenomena. The reports are accompanied by physics demonstration experiments, which are prepared and explained by students themselves. Let us focus on some experiments. Firstly, there are experiments demonstrating the formation of soap films on frames of various shapes. In all cases, the film takes the form of a minimum surface area; this observation is visual evidence to the energy interpretation of the surface tension coefficient and should lead students to the conclusion that the system tends to the minimum value of potential energy. Secondly, there are experiments with soap films on reducing their surface area, illustrating the effect of surface tension forces. Having observed the movable lower side on a metal frame beginning to move up after being dipped into a soap solution, you can calculate the work of surface tension forces and consider the force interpretation of the surface tension coefficient.

In this form of training, students turn from passive receivers into active participants in the educational process. The introduction of interactive learning technology allows creating conditions in which students themselves will discover, acquire, and analyze knowledge. The apparent simplicity of the experiments should not depreciate researchers' merits, as the researchers are first-year undergraduate students, who also have to overcome the psychological barrier, speaking to a large audience of their fellow students.

Students' Development of Working Models of Devices that Demonstrate Physical Phenomena and Processes

Students can acquire useful practical skills in physics by designing models of physical devices. To present their work, students need to be knowledgeable in the physical phenomena, processes, and laws that underlie the operation of devices, to carry out literary and technological design and information support of research results, for example, in the form of a presentation or a report. Models created by students can be used to demonstrate physical phenomena during seminars and lectures. The most interesting experimental setups can later be used as exhibits in the Museum of the Institute of Physics and Technology.

As an example, let us consider Van de Graaff's model of an electrostatic generator and the model of Kelvin's water dropper. At the lecture in "Electricity and magnetism" when studying the charge distribution on the conductor surface, students get acquainted with the fact that by reiterating the charge transfer to a hollow conductor, it is possible to significantly increase its potential. They learn that this principle was used by Van de Graaff in 1929 to build an electrostatic generator, a device in which a high DC voltage is created by the mechanical transfer of electric charges. Students are asked to make a model of such a generator. Fig. (**1a**) shows the model of Van de Graaff's electrostatic generator, made at home by first-year students. Inside the vertical plastic tube there is a dielectric (rubber) belt, mounted on two rollers, which are driven by an electric motor from a child's toy. Through a metal comb the upper conductive metal can is in contact with the moving belt. It is clear that in terms of technical characteristics this model is inferior to the reference standard, and the novice experimenter was not able to obtain a high potential difference, however, when the device is in operation, it is possible to make sure that the charge is accumulated by the deviation of the paper strips on the upper metal can.

a)

b)

Fig. (1). Photographs of students' experimental models: **a)** the model of Van de Graaff generator, **b)** the model of Kelvin water dropper.

Students were also asked to assemble the model of a Kelvin water dropper to generate electricity from water. Despite the large amount of information in the

Internet and the external simplicity of the devices, the manufacture of a model that enabled to observe noticeable and stable effects required considerable effort from students. For example, in order to assemble a Kelvin generator model (see Fig. **1b**), you need to use a reservoir with non-distilled water with two holes (or two containers connected by a conductor), which is kept at a height. Two streams of water from the upper containers flow through the copper rings and fall into metal cans connected to the copper rings (the right ring is connected to the left can and the left ring to the right can). The task of the experiment was to figure out what effects the generator could demonstrate, namely, the charge accumulation in lower metal cans, the occurrence of potential differences between these cans, and the achievability to observe these effects. Students' experimental models demonstrated the possibility to observe the splitting of the water stream into drops near copper rings, the periodic occurrence of a spark between copper wires, and the flashing of a neon bulb connected to the lower can. Students also checked how the composition of water (tap water, salted water, spring water) affects the quality of the observed effects. For the presentation of their work students needed to understand better the physical phenomena, processes and laws that underlie the operation of the devices: such as the charge interaction, electrification of bodies, the behavior of conductors and dielectrics in an electric field, safety measures when working with electrostatic devices.

Students' Research on Physical Topics

There are topics to study that are assigned to first-year students within their project work, which involve physical and applied problems. For example, the topics include the issues: "Standing waves", "Heat engines", "Physics of the pipe organ". One of the most favorable topics among students is "Physics in movie mistakes". Creative assignments for this topic provoked a special audience response. The authors of the assignments showed some excerpts from films and explained inconsistencies on the screen from a physical perspective. For example, while demonstrating some episodes of the films "Star Wars" and "Gravity", students showed the classic inconsistencies associated with the sound accompanying the movement of a spacecraft in space, obvious violations in the law of momentum conservation during the movement of astronauts. And then they examined more complex episodes when the main character of "Indiana Jones" movie rushed at a huge speed in an open cart, and when the cart stopped abruptly, the character could easily maintain his balance. It is difficult to find a better way to illustrate the inertial forces as was demonstrated in the video. Such topics appeared to be a good solution to engage even less motivated students to study physics.

ORGANIZATION OF INTERDISCIPLINARY PROJECT WORK

Another area of our work was the organization of interdisciplinary research within the framework of project activities, integrating such disciplines as physics, mathematics and a foreign language. We develop project topics at the intersection of these disciplines so that students could apply the acquired knowledge in their projects. Analyzing the subject matter of each project, the authors identified the mathematical and physical parts, the latter, in turn, consisted of theoretical and experimental parts [2, 7, 10, 11].

Now we would like to dwell upon the importance of the mathematical part in projects, its role in the formation of the mathematical and research competence of a future graduate. By mathematical competence we understand the integrative property of a personality determined by a complex of mathematical abilities, knowledge, skills, creative abilities, volitional and reflective personality traits, and manifested in the willingness to successfully apply them in a professional sphere [12].

Let us discuss one of the projects in more detail. The measurement of physical quantities and obtaining their numerical values are an essential task of most physical experiments. But the results of all measurements, no matter how carefully they are performed, are always obtained with some errors. The ability to work with errors is an important part of any scientific experiment at all its stages, as well as at the stage of interpreting the results of an experiment or an observation. But without accuracy of measurements and without correct statistical processing, it is impossible to draw reasonable conclusions in a particular physical model or hypothesis. That is why, as one of the topics we proposed the following: "Modeling a random error by weighing in a laboratory experiment".

Students were required to study independently some issues of probability theory and mathematical statistics as part of their project work, since the discipline "Probability theory" is studied only in the second year. The theoretical part of the project includes such concepts as probability, the law of random distribution, probability density, distribution parameters, the statistical universe and the sample, the normal distribution, the correlation coefficient, and testing the hypothesis about the compliance of sample distribution to the normal law. The experimental part involved mass measurement of a single coin, as well as processing and analyzing the data.

Students carried out a series of measurements and calculations of the coin mass as part of their experimental work. Statistical processing of measurements was conducted in Excel. Based on the data obtained, histograms were constructed, the parameters of the estimated normal distribution were measured, sample means and variance, correlation coefficients were calculated. The graphical method of analyzing weighing results allowed us to put forward a hypothesis about the normal distribution law of weighing errors. The work with the results of several samples allowed us to offer recommendations for the selection of the sample size to check the normal distribution law of a random variable in a laboratory practicum.

Students whose projects were successful prepared their presentations for the Scientific Conference for students, graduate students and young scientists, which is annually held at PetrSU. While preparing for the reports, first-year students develop public speech skills, try to understand the topic deeper and adjust the results of their activities to real situations, obtain the opportunity to assess their achievements adequately with the help of self and mutual assessment.

Modern science has become international, that is why teaching students English as a language of international scientific communication is of great importance nowadays. To integrate different professional skills, the professors of the Institute of Physics and Technology of PetrSU organize a section in English within the Scientific Students Conference in which students can present the results of their first scientific research in English. Here are some topics of first-year students at the foreign language section of the conference:

1. Quantum computers: principles of work.
2. The use of computer vision in industry.
3. The use of information and computer technologies in modern education.
4. Artificial intelligence: problems and prospects.
5. Jet motion and Meshchersky's equation.
6. Semiconductors in the world of modern materials.
7. Problems of classical physics.
8. Newton's classical gravitation theory.
9. Doppler's effect in classical physics.
10. The effect of radiation on humans and the environment.

Students' engagement in a scientific student conference in a foreign language allows them to be more easily involved in the work of the international scientific student community later.

Besides, the development of professional foreign language competencies is facilitated by the study of specialized literature in a foreign language which includes the search for information and building text skills. In the process of working with professional foreign language texts, students learn to use professional vocabulary in a foreign language, analyze graphs and schemes, describe basic physical formulas and laws, explain physical phenomena, and write essays about the results of their physical experiments. Another example of active learning in a foreign language class at a technical university can be the creation of video films in a foreign language in which students demonstrate the results of their experimental work in physics.

CONCLUSION

Thus, education of highly qualified engineers that can ensure the sufficient level of competence in professional spheres should primarily be based on a solid foundation of natural science in such disciplines as physics and mathematics. The joint efforts of the authors of the article were aimed at providing students with a sustainable, rather than episodic, involvement in the educational process, increasing motivation and creating a comfortable psychological learning environment which helps to acquire the first experience of independent research work.

Active learning methods described in the article such as the project-based learning, interdisciplinary interaction, interactive learning, the organization of seminars with physical demonstrations, creation of video clips, digital-stories are used in physics, mathematics and foreign language classes to carry out the educational process of engineering specialists more effectively. The methods shape the needs for obtaining and applying practical knowledge at these subjects, contribute to the development of creative potential and research skills of students.

CONSENT FOR PUBLICATION

Not applicable.

CONFLICT OF INTEREST

The authors declare no conflict of interest, financial or otherwise.

ACKNOWLEDGEMENTS

Declared none.

REFERENCES

[1] C. von Aufschnaiter, and S. von Aufschnaiter, "University students' activities, thinking and learning during laboratory work", *Eur. J. Phys.*, vol. 28, 2007.
[http://dx.doi.org/10.1088/0143-0807/28/3/S05]

[2] C. Michelsen, "Mathematical modeling is also physics – interdisciplinary teaching between mathematics and physics in Danish upper secondary education", *Phys. Educ.*, vol. 50, no. 4, pp. 489-494, 2015.
[http://dx.doi.org/10.1088/0031-9120/50/4/489]

[3] R.M.D. Guido, "Attitude and Motivation towards Learning Physics", *Int. J. Eng. Res. Technol. (Ahmedabad),* vol. 2, no. 11, 2013.

[4] L.C. Hodges, Student Engagement in Active Learning Classes.*Active Learning in College Science* Springer: Cham, 2020, pp. 27-41.
[http://dx.doi.org/10.1007/978-3-030-33600-4_3]

[5] J.J.B. Harlow, D. Harrison, and A. Meyertholen, "Effective student teams for collaborative learning in an introductory university physics course", *Physical Review Physics Education Research,* vol. 12, 2016p. 010138. journals.aps.org
[http://dx.doi.org/10.1103/PhysRevPhysEducRes.12.010138]

[6] B.E. Penprase, *STEM Education for the 21st Century.* Springer: Cham, 2020.
[http://dx.doi.org/10.1007/978-3-030-41633-1]

[7] E. Kazakova, M. Kruchek, E. Moshkina, O. Sergeeva, and E. Tikhomirova, "Interdisciplinary approach to the study of physics and mathematical analysis", *In: ICERI2019 Proceedings,* pp. 4196-4201, 2019.
[http://dx.doi.org/10.21125/iceri.2019.1046]

[8] M. Marušić, and J. Sliško, "High-school students believe school physics helps in developing logical but not creative thinking: active learning can change this idea", *European Journal of Physics Education,* vol. 5, no. 4, pp. 30-41, 2017.

[9] R.I. Btemirova, "Method of projects in the modern higher education", *Modern problems of science and education,* no. 3, p. 217, 2016. www.science-education.ru

[10] W.A. Widakdo, "Mathematical representation ability by using project based learning on the topic of statistics", *J. Phys. Conf. Ser.,* vol. 895, 2017.
[http://dx.doi.org/10.1088/1742-6596/895/1/012055]

[11] E. V. Moshkina, E. L. Kazakova, M. M. Kruchek, and O. V. Sergeeva, "Aspects of the organization of the educational process in physics and mathematical analysis within the framework of an interdisciplinary approach", *Physical education in universities,* no. 2, pp. 30-40, 2018.

[12] F. Dilling, I. Stricker, T.N. Chat, and V.D. Phuong, Development of Knowledge in Mathematics and Physics Education.*Comparison of Mathematics and Physics Education I* Springer Spektrum: Wiesbaden, 2020, pp. 299-344.
[http://dx.doi.org/10.1007/978-3-658-29880-7_13]

CHAPTER 3

Can Physics Education Support A Self-Responsible Society?

Gilbert Ahamer[1,*]

[1] Karl-Franzens University Graz, Institute for Economic and Social History, Universitätsstrasse 15/F2, 8010 Graz, Austria

Abstract: In the face of the "European Green Deal", our continent needs young cohorts of self-responsible citizens steering the globe towards responsible sustainability.

This article reflects two didactic approaches for strengthening self-responsibility in students: the approach "3 x 7 = 21" and the approach "jet principle". Both rely on dialogue and confrontation of learners with their peers – often a more stringent educational agent that contact with teachers.

The very simple method "3 x 7 = 21" sets learners into 3 phases of iterative complexity: single achievements, groups of 3 and groups of 7 while they iteratively exchange their views on complex interdisciplinary subjects.

The more elaborated method "jet principle" leads learners into framework conditions which they actually formed during their previous steps: analogous to a jet turbine, the border conditions of subsequent learning stages are the result of energetic applications of confrontations during earlier stages.

Both methods are suitable for advanced physics students in any transdisciplinary setting.

Keywords: "3 x 7 = 21", Curriculum, Dialogic learning, Discursive learning, Globalization, Global studies, Global studies consortium, Graz University, Interparadigmatic, Jet principle, Quality assurance, Transdisciplinary.

INTRODUCTION

This article presents two didactic methods, namely "3 x 7 = 21" and the "Jet Principle", based on a pedagogy of dialogue and discourse [1 - 5].

---

[*] **Corresponding author Gilbert Ahamer:** Karl-Franzens University Graz, Institute for Economic and Social History, Universitätsstrasse 15/F2, 8010 Graz, Austria; E-mail: gilbert.ahamer@uni-graz.at

Maria Teresa Caccamo and Salvatore Magazù (Eds.)
All rights reserved-© 2021 Bentham Science Publishers

For ten years, these and similar didactic approaches were implemented at several universities and produced a series of collaborative student articles published by students and collaborative student reports which document the results of the described didactic approaches [6 - 25].

PHYSICS LABS FIRST DIDACTIC METHOD "3×7 = 21"

Didactic Basics of the Course Design "3×7 = 21"

Based on the challenges posed by "global change", this article proposes to train discourses in universities on how to develop a consensus that is as sustainable (*i.e.* durable and environmentally oriented) as possible, namely based on sound, interdisciplinary expertise.

A suitable rhythmised process design of consensus development includes formulating and rethinking everybody's own point of view and then "weaving" it into an overall consensus.

This concrete course strategy means interdisciplinary training in a "3 x 7 = 21" architecture which creates changing intradisciplinary and interdisciplinary encounters among learners. The method "3 x 7 = 21" fills the theoretical requirements of a dialogical and discursive didactic approach with real life and on a practical level provides cooperative seminar papers by students on individual and a collective bases which may also be used for assessment of students' achievements including very targeted grading. For universities, the overall question is how best to respond to "global change" and to take into account its environmental impact, but also its social and economic structural changes. Thus, in general, this innovative method can be carried out well in courses where students from different disciplines (and from different countries of origin) come together.

Considering Several Value Systems Means An Inter-Paradigmatic Approach

Stepwise approaches to complex inter-paradigmatic problems such as global (climate) change are useful when divided into single days with individual, then intradisciplinary collaboration, then interdisciplinary collaboration, as explained in the following example of a course plan established with "3 x 7 = 21" didactics.

At first, each teacher of a team of teachers or lecturers starts with teaching their own basic concepts as perceived by each presenter. In practice, this may be a block of 2 hours for each lecturer. Then, the students carry out their own written work assignment or (literature) search on a selectable subtopic of the overall theme (*e.g.* technical, geographic, economic, or social aspects of global warming). This written work is presented (*e.g.via* an online learning platform), then discussed face-to-face during the 2 hours of a subsequent university course and then these views are balanced within the group of colleagues.

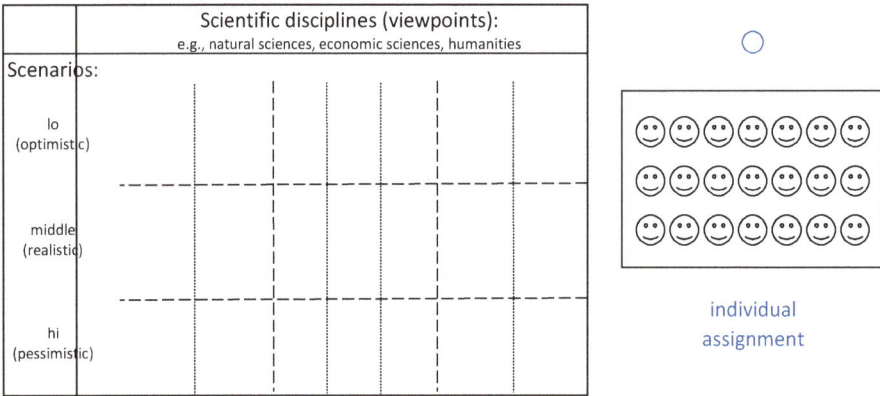

Fig. (1). Matrix-like overall structure of a "3 x 7 = 21" course: 3 groups of disciplines (according to those of the lecturers but also the students, horizontal) and three scenario inclinations (vertical).

In a next step of work, the students discuss and revise their work in intra- and interdisciplinary dialogue with the appropriate accompaniment of lecturers (see the diagrams in Figs. (**1** to **3**)). Then follows an in-depth block by each lecturer; these may clarify in-depth questions which emerged as a result of student discussions. Thereby, all advantages of e-learning are made use of on all levels of communication, namely content provision, discussion forums, online quizzes and mutual feedback.

The Concrete Didactic Process of "3 x 7 = 21"

Through the characteristic organizational structure in groups, the concrete didactic procedure develops step by step as follows:

- Generation of empathy and collection of the emotional impressions (anonymous, *via* the learning platform) in order to determine where the students should be "picked up" emotionally, and what their initial level of knowledge is.
- Then there should come one block by each specialised lecturer, in which each lecturer presents material & content (*e.g.* as a PowerPoint or oral presentation,

which should then be made available on the learning platform). This first conveyance of basic knowledge should enable the students to work on information sources critically and thus acquire knowledge independently by themselves.
- Students (who often might amount to groups of some twenty, in practice) choose from 21 roughly predetermined topics (7x3 = 21), while each student might prefer to choose from their own earlier speciality and area of interest. Everyone is personally involved. It is important that these assignments are written individual assignments, namely for the purpose of awarding grades later. The motto is: 1 topic per person.
- First, each student produces an individual piece of written work, namely a professionally argued opinion based on scientific evidence (which is at the core of every modern society – or at least should be), based on their own research of (partly web-based) literature. Each student posts this work in a dedicated discussion forum in the learning platform. The topic may be taken from one of the seven subject groups that cover the lecturers' specialties and moreover adopts one of three basic attitudes (optimistic, realistic, pessimistic). See Fig. (**1**).
- In brief: 1 topic / person. Posting on the web platform. Oral presentation may be possible later.

In a next step, seven discipline-oriented groups are formed, if possible, according to the previous knowledge (or specialisation) of students. An example is the curriculum of Environmental Systems Science at Graz University in Austria, disposing of several specialities, namely business administration, economics, geography, physics, chemistry [26 - 28]. Another example is the interdepartmental Master's degree in Global Studies at universities in Graz or Salzburg, Austria. Again, there are 3 scenarios (*i.e.*, basic inclinations of opinions expressed) within each discipline, which should be differentiated and justified in the next version of the written assignment (leave 2 weeks working time).

The following steps boil down to a stepwise (collaborative, non-competitive) process of iteratively updating these student assignments, namely first vertically and second horizontally within the matrix in Fig. (**1**). This iterative procedure is led, moderated and accompanied by a leading senior lecturer (who should be very experienced in transdisciplinary work and should overlook the entire academic field, mostly the one organising the entire transdisciplinary course) while taking care of technical and argumentative balance in order to obtain well-rounded scientific statements.

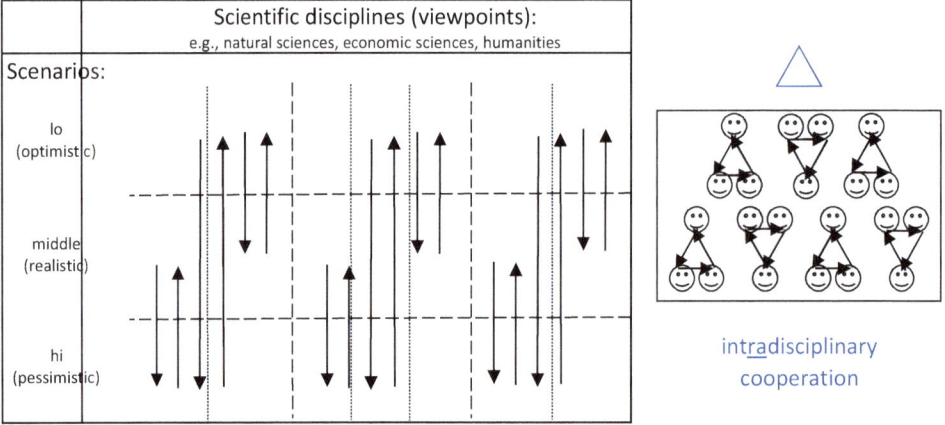

Fig. (2). Intradisciplinary collaboration in the 1st revision of the individual points of view.

First, after two working weeks, there is the exchange of "homonymous" students intradisciplinary exchange (Fig. **2**), who should make the arguments consistent, clarify, condense and countercheck them.

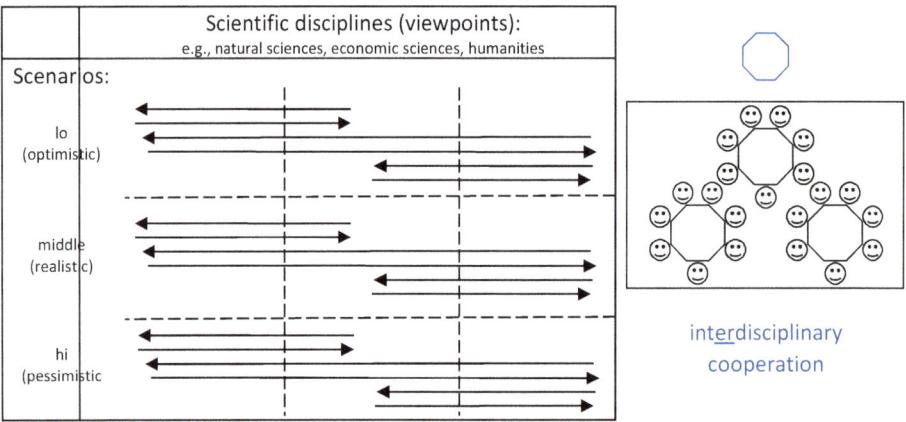

Fig. (3). Interdisciplinary cooperation in the 2nd revision of the individual points of view. The octogon symbolizes the seven students.

After another week of work, there comes the exchange among "dissimilar" students, namely those within the same type of scenario interdisciplinary exchange (Fig. **3**), which is intended to clarify scenario assumptions and effects, while the seven students sit together on three tables and each creates an interdisciplinary overall report. In this step, the entire interdisciplinary spectrum is spanned by all those involved.

Due to this course structure, a gradual, horizontal and vertical "weaving" process should emerge as well as an analogue social dynamic among students.

This is followed by an in-depth content presentation in front of the entire class which actually establishes *interdisciplinary connections*. After an at least two-week break, the students hence present their final version in the plenum.

Reflection of the "3 x 7 = 21" Process

Summing up, this article tries to substantiate the terms of dialogical and discursive didactics, to provide practical examples and to examine their application at universities. For the university, the question arises as to how to react appropriately to "global change" and to take into account its environmental impact, but also its social and economic structural changes.

The didactic method "3 x 7 = 21" described again in Table **1** shows that:

- the perception of different and even conflicting viewpoints and partial truths of a technically complex problem can be enhanced by dialogues in different constellations.
- web support is a suitable vehicle for enabling and enhancing of actions in dialogue in which an increased density of communication can occur (up to about 1000 hits / course).
- review processes between peer students are possible in highest detail when using the discussion forum functionality of a web platform, because students work when and where they prefer, and can apply time for in-depth analysis of their comrades' work.
- this appropriate rhythm of learning and communication offers several phases in the overall formation of successive writing: intermediate results can facilitate preliminary understanding on which subsequent steps can build.
- even this simple "dramaturgy" of a university course (such as "3 x 7 = 21") is preferable in the eyes of students and lecturers because it enables more interesting and intensive events, as is proven by anonymous feedback at course end.
- NGOs as crystallization nuclei of civil society could play an even stronger exemplary role in the future, for which in turn universities should prepare appropriately.

- the didactic concept of "discourse" can harmonise very well with the philosophical and epistemological views of American pragmatism, as evidenced by a literature search [29 - 31].

Finally, university practice is encouraged to understand and be active as a "training camp" for technically grounded civil society discursive and dialogical behaviour of the fellow citizens.

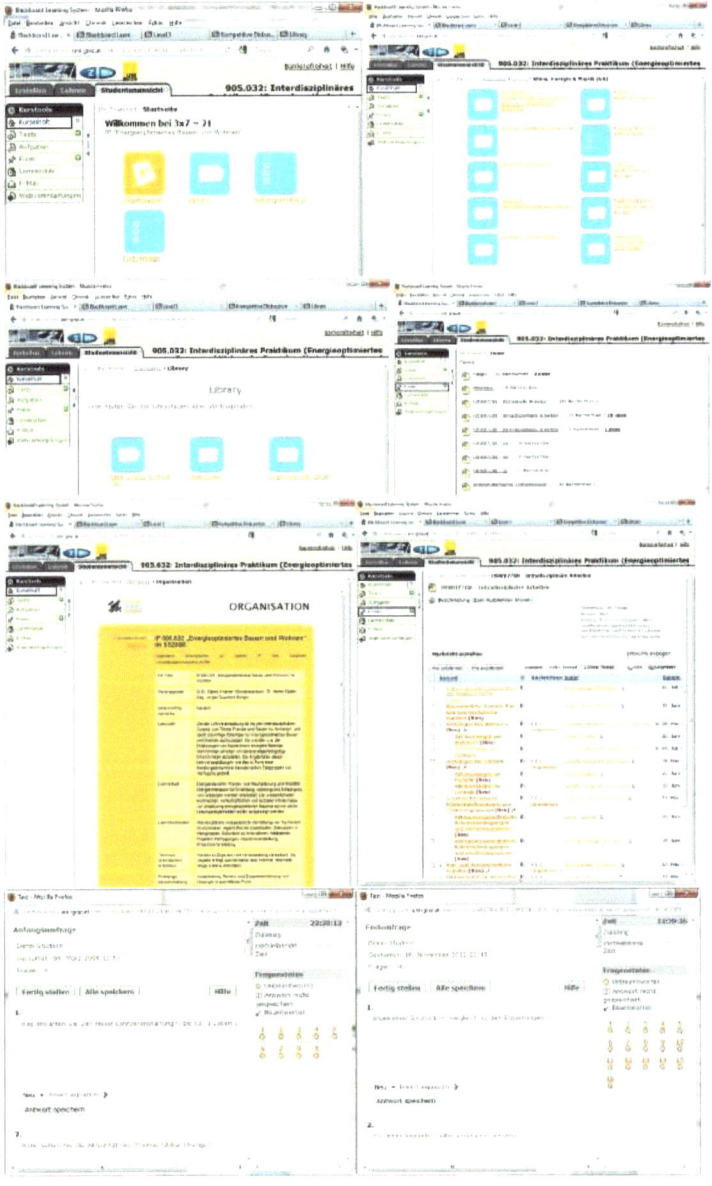

Fig. (4). Implementation of "3 x 7 = 21" at Graz University for students of Environmental Systems Sciences.

Table 1. Details of the teaching method "3 x 7 = 21".

Title	"3 x 7 = 21"
Overview of this teaching method	*Structure*: Students write and review seminar papers according to the following scheme: first one individual work, then one work in groups of three, then one in groups of seven. The actual numbers can be modified if there are not around 21 students participating. *Objectives*: Transdisciplinary action and assessment competence for complex topics. *Contents*: Technical justification in the transdisciplinary dialogue of three future perspectives (optimistic – realistic – pessimistic) with regard to several disciplines or topics.
Recommended course type:	Interdisciplinary course with 4 weekly hours and three lecturers. *Introductory*: Retrieval of the emotional status (anonymous, *via* web platform) to determine where the students should be "picked up", *i.e.* their initial level of opinion and knowledge. In contrast to this initial status, the progress in the course of the course could be measured later at the end stage. *At the Beginning, there* should be 1 block in which each lecturer presents material and content (*e.g.* as a PowerPoint presentation, which should be available on the web platform). This should enable the students to critically work on information sources and thus acquire knowledge independently and themselves. *First step*: Students choose from twentyish given topics (3 x 7 = 21), and each student from their own subject area (corresponding to their individual study area). Each person deals personally with a portion of the overall topic. It is important that these are written individual works. Maintaining the three scenarios (optimistic, realistic, pessimistic – because this reflects three basic attitudes in many environmentally related perceptions of the future) each of the subject areas represented by the lecturers is represented by three scenarios (*i.e.*, future perspectives in order to be able to measure the range of the possible "future"). Hence, course structure as provided in Fig. (**1**). *Second step*: Then, seven discipline-oriented groups are formed, if possible, according to the main areas of study. That would give 3 x 7 = 21 students. There are 3 scenarios in each discipline-oriented group, which should be differentiated and justified (allow 2 weeks working time for the students).

(Table 1) cont.....

-	Then a stepwise (collaborative, non-competitive) reviewing/updating process by students follows, namely transversely and longitudinally on the matrix in Fig. (**1**). This is led, moderated and accompanied by an experienced senior lecturer with strong transdisciplinary profile, taking care of technical and argumentative balance in order to obtain well-equilibrated student statements. After two working weeks, there is the exchange of "homonymous" students (*intra*-disciplinary exchange, (Fig. **2**), which should make arguments consistent, clarify, condense and countercheck. ***Third** step*: Thereafter, another exchange occurs after a further week of work "heteronymous" students within the same type of scenario (*inter*-disciplinary exchange, (Fig. **3**), in which i.a. the scenario assumptions and scenario impacts are to be clarified. Because of this course structure, a stepwise, transversally and longitudinally woven *process of equilibration of views* is achieved on the *factual* level and an analogous *pattern of social dynamics* is achieved on the *social* level. An in-depth content-related presentation follows at course end including solicitation of interactive questions and critical discussions, which establishes interdisciplinary connections. After an at least two-week break, the students present their final version in the plenum.
Relation to sustainability	*Ecological sustainability*: Topics are mostly chosen for questions related to environmental protection because the logical chain structure corresponds to the "*common thread of the greenhouse effect*", namely: economy => emission => immission => climate change or more generally the DPSIR concept of the EU / EEA: drivers – pressure – state – impact – response. *Social sustainability*: Repeated review processes create a common perspective between the different authors and thus a high probability that consensus will actually be reached.
Learning goals	The learning objective is the *overall* understanding of a higher-level chain of effects, *e.g.* the greenhouse effect, and not just that of a single topic. Furthermore, the perception of other, often different points of view as well as the incorporation of constructive criticism into your own world view and your own seminar work.
Group size	~21 students
Time required	1 semester; each course having > 90 minutes, best 4 weekly hours It is best to use it as a script for a course that spans the entire semester, then there is enough time for sufficient technical expertise.
Didactic description of the teaching method	*Interdisciplinary learning* *Supported competencies*: professional competence, ability to change perspectives, action competence, communicative competence, organizational competence, self-competence, teamwork. *Information and communication media*: Learning platform: Almost any learning platform can be used flexibly, provided that it has a discussion forum (with options for attachments) and provides sufficient content.
Evaluation	Because of the initially individual work as well as the subsequent team work and the final collective versions of the work, grading is feasible on all levels.

Possible content	For environment-oriented and development-oriented studies: for example, "Interdisciplinary internships", for example with the title "World in Change? – Comparison of three socio-economic, climatic & technological future perspectives", other courses see under literature.

Web Design for "3 x 7 = 21"

The above-placed Fig. (**4**) provides visual impressions of a possible web-based implementation.

SECOND DIDACTIC METHOD: THE JET PRINCIPLE IN E-LEARNING

Introduction and Motivation for the "Jet Principle"

The – often surprising – conclusion of many interdisciplinary and multicultural projects and lectures is that providing views on reality is essential, namely mediation among different and diverse perspectives of realities. Such attempts can be very crucial in cases of disagreement on what "real truth" is, *e.g.* in cases of fundamentally different approaches mediated by religion [32, 33] or globalisation.

Each human action can be seen as taking place and creating effects on several factual, personal, or strategic levels at a time. It is the core task of teachers to care for all these levels simultaneously. Trainers and pedagogues should thus reach consistent, valid and lasting learning results [34, 35].

The learning strategy and didactic procedure presented in this article, the "*jet principle*", will later give rise to comparing any enhanced learning endeavour with a jet engine: the walls of the combustion chamber mean the learning framework, and the accelerated gas masses represent the learning activities.

Social procedures should be professionally designed in a way so as to allow for convergence of opposing world views, be it for spatial planning, peace negotiations [36], environment or development. The breadth and scope of the (public) perception of realities [37], appears as a decisive bottleneck for the durability and ability to implement sustainable solutions. Example: Regarding a Caucasian conflict, Huseynov [38] says that "as a result of these perceptions, the dynamism in the peace process (…) does not resonate well with the wider population".

Fig. (5). Any (social or learning) process takes place on several personal, political, economic, developmental, cultural, communicational or strategic layers at a time and each action in one layer is connected to simultaneous actions on other layers. Concrete examples for such interlinked layers are the three parameters selected in Fig. (**6**).

Understanding the Design of the "Jet Principle"

The web-based "jet principle" (SGC, Fig. **6**) is one example of a structured dialogue using discussions for a theme that allows taking and understanding opposing views.

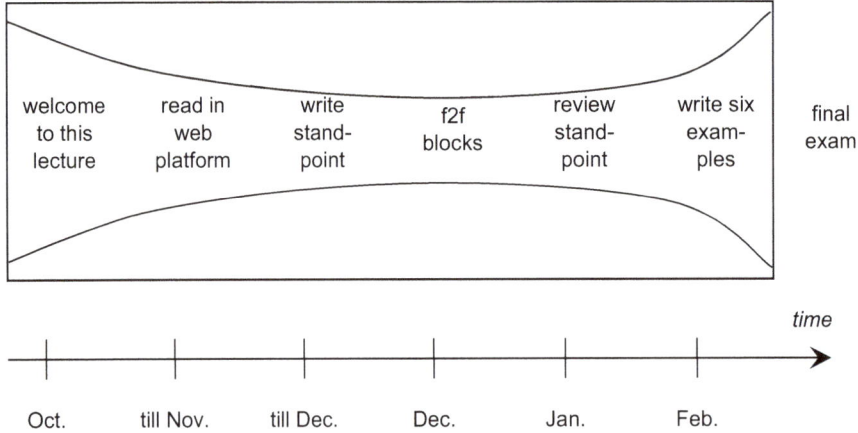

Fig. (6). The "jet principle" design of learning embraces some six consecutive elements of learning, authoring and revising standpoints.

The practice of a lecture using the "jet principle" [39] during one semester shows a highly interactive and communicative social process (around thousand web clicks per student and per semester).

Inventing a "Jet Engine" for Smoothing Learning Processes

Seen from a physical and technological point of view, a jet engine accelerates gas particles in an optimal manner. As a principle, an engineer's mechanical design sequentially arranges distinct parts of machinery. Such a geometric structure produces distinct but well-defined aerodynamic regimes along sections of the horizontal axis (Fig. **7**). A jet engine hence consists of identifiably designed building blocks resulting in a smoothly accelerating mass flow.

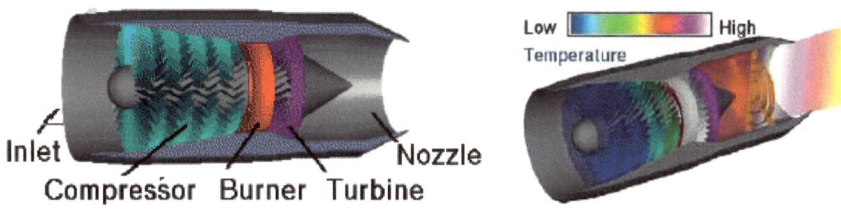

Fig. (7). The composition of a jet turbine shows distinct mechanical parts. Image source [40].

We use this array of design in mechanical engineering as a symbol for the *design of social border conditions during learning* in a university course that might employ the five phases of action in the "Global Studies" lecture or any other dialogic design enhancing self-responsibility. SGC defines distinct social procedures along the numbered levels.

We interpret the vertical axis of Fig. (**7**) as "tightness of *structures*" in the mechanical sense, which translates to "a corset by *rules*" in the social sense. As Fig. (**8**) suggests, the social flow of "jet engine"-like learning has the same design as a jet engine, namely gradually and smoothly tightening border conditions, while allowing results to develop in an unrestricted manner. This is demonstrated by the curbed lines in Fig. (**8**), which we can – at first sight – interpret as "degree of freedom" for the participants of the course. The reader will match the "social actions" in the course expressed in technological terms in the central row of Fig. (**8**) with the learning and gaming actions described in Fig. (**6**) – or in more detail in the game rules. The gas stream in a jet turbine (and generally any dynamic process described by a system of differential equations) is largely defined by external forcing (*e.g.* geometrical shape of the jet) and by the fundamental laws, theoretically by the ideal gas law (p.V = ν.R.T).

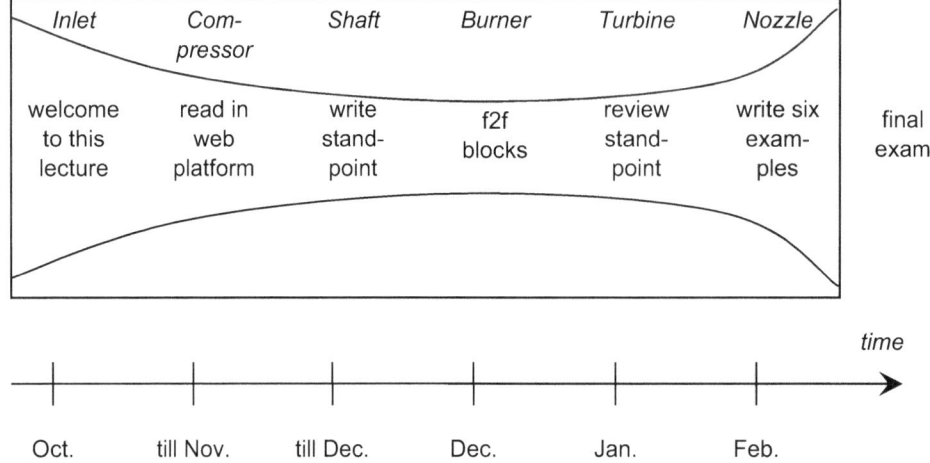

Fig. (8). The setup and social design of learning activities follows the design of a jet engine. The phases symbolically compare to the design of a jet engine. The vertical axis denotes the tightness of structures in both cases. Source: own design.

Similarly, any learning and teaching indicates the suitable design in and of these substrates: *time*, *space* as well as possibly *structures* in a more general way.

Symbolic Interpretation of the Analogy with a Jet Engine

The jet engine was invented in the second half of the 1930s and exhibits some features that can also be made use of in learning and teaching – if these features are interpreted in a symbolic manner.

A very decisive technological innovation consisted in replacing the four-stroke cycle engine of an internal combustion engine (first column in Table **2**) with a jet engine (second column in Table **2**). The earlier engineering concept of "each (combustion) phase has its proper place in time and space" was replaced by the jet concept "as a package of air proceeds through the installation, it is led into suitable boundary conditions for performing the foreseen procedures". Instead of revolving pistons separating the flow of time into four distinct phases located in geometrically well-defined chambers with four distinct border conditions of pressure, volume and temperature, where one phase explicitly "hands over" the system state into the next phase (by moving its material parts, namely the piston); in the jet engine one and the same material installation (with still standing parts) allows the procedure to pass through.

Whereas in a traditional approach matter had to move in order to squeeze the process through, in later approaches matter stood still and allowed the process to "flow" along its appropriately designed wall structure. We will call this fundamental idea the "jet principle" explained in detail in Table 2.

Table 2. Comparison of joint features in engineering (left two columns) and in education (two columns to the far right). For both of these disciplines the traditional approach is always found at left and the progressive approach always at right.

In Engineering		In Education	
Four Stroke Engine	**Jet Engine**	**Traditional Education**	**The "Jet Principle" Education**
Closed combustion chamber	Open-ended combustion chamber	Closed learning setting	Open learning process setting
Combustion finished when piston at far point	Combustion finished when gas has left jet area	Act of cognition successful, when issue is "learned"	There is no final state of knowing that can be "learned"
Result is properly working through the "stroke"	Result is equal to preparation for the next phase	Result in exam is underlined by double line	Result is maximum step forward measured from step in advance
Matter acts	Stream acts	Content orientation	Process orientation
Design lies in geometrically co-ordinating moving combustion room	Design lies in physically co-ordinating gas properties	Design lies in feeding students with proper learning material	Design lies in letting students' autopoietic hunger come into force
Concomitance through connecting rod and axis	Concomitance through engine walls and axis	Concomitance: one teacher acts for different students simultaneously	Concomitance: one student acts on different levels simultaneously
Four distinct phases impressed from the "outside"	Sequence of phases, one evolving from the other	Discontinuous process: asking and answering	Continuous process: learning from iterative situations
Boundary conditions stamped on from outside by camshaft	Boundary conditions result from preceding phase state	Learning objective imposed from outside teacher or curriculum	Learning objective formed by student: constructivist, autopoietic, self-responsible

The "jet engine" learning design is a booster, not a final solver; it is a problem handling jet.

The "jet engine" learning design channels perceptions of issues in a transitory way and frees them again after compression.

The "Jet Principle" in (E-)Learning

The "jet principle" has revolutionised air traffic in the middle of the 20th century.

Let us therefore generalise from Table **2** a "jet principle" in learning that can be implemented for most themes; and still more easily when exploiting the technological opportunities provided by e-learning. The reader may form his or her own (additional) interpretation based on their personal experiences; here are some suggestions:

Jet design means impressing a structure onto a process in such a way that it allows for suitable evolution. The first effect is a deeper understanding, namely to perceive an array and *sequence of interlaced necessary procedures* to cope with the initial problem, namely a "structured problem" and create awareness for it in the participants. There is a scientific discipline which has long been dealing with such issues, namely design science (see its literature, *e.g.* Journal of Design Research, Design Studies) and levels of expertise [41]. Restrepo and Christiaans [42] speak of "ill-defined problems" and write that problem structuring occurs mainly in the design process but also reoccurs periodically as the design activity progresses.

This is a good argument for needing an iterative structure of learning and teaching in which the learners stemming from different conceptual cultures are called in to find their targets, themes, case studies and discussion partners in responsibility-led self-control and autonomous target-setting; independent of their initial stage of skills. Such is the deep intention of the "jet principle" and this should additionally be the principle of any "development cooperation".

In learning, everybody principally has a different starting point (predefined by age, preceding experience or studies, and the culture of understanding to date), hence the *relative increase of skills* during a seminar should be maximised. Similarly, a jet engine takes in any air parcels irrespective of their initial speed – it always boosts and *accelerates these air parcels in a maximal manner* after having passed them through the array of border conditions called "jet engine".

A hypothesis:

(economically and ecologically) *sustainable results* <= (socially) *sustainable procedures*

These above deliberations are applicable to a) individual learning (*e.g.* students on a course on climate change or on peace keeping), b) societal learning (*e.g.* a nation implementing new democratic or sustainable regimes).

Both exhibit analogous phases and periods in their learning processes.

When listening to system scientists [43] it becomes clear that the decision between "intended main effect" and "undesired side effect" merely exists on the screen of our fundamentally flawed cognitive map. Intrinsically, all effects occur regardless of whether we label them "intended or not". As a consequence for learning, the deep social involvement of learners has to be taken into account. Concomitance (see Table **2**) has to be cared for.

The author suggests the "jet principle" of learning to improve learning results.

Description of the "Jet Principle" Process

The following paragraphs and images provide a quick introduction on what this principle means in concrete terms.

The target of such implementation is to create an important amount of student activity with a small number of weekly hours of lecture.

Each student – apart from performing the normal learning path of studying the lecture notes and passing the written exam – may make use of the opportunity to write a written assignment and to review the assignments of 2 colleagues. Additional to this option of writing a standpoint, students may also write short texts on a maximum of 6 examples ("Ex"). The result in all cases is much higher quality and student performance.

"Global Studies" is a discursive process encouraging multiple paradigms: This multicultural venue of learners was dynamically structured by a web discourse (Fig. **6**).

For the purpose of this text, the following definitions are made:

a. inter*disciplinary*: to look at n facets of reality (*e.g.* physics, chemistry, meteorology regarding climate change).
b. inter*cultural*: to view reality from m standpoints (according to the roles of the actors defining different viewing angles, *e.g.* as Armenian or Azerbaijani on Nagorno-Karabakh, compare BBC (2010) [44], Global Security (2010)) [45].
c. inter*paradigmatic*: the combination of the above, namely to look at n facets of reality from m viewing angles (logically a n:m relationship).

The author's share of the GS curriculum (which has been defined as *multiparadigmatic*) covers for example "Social and Cultural Geography", a recent branch of human geography that strongly adopts a *multiparadigmatic* stance [46 - 50]. During its genesis, human geography has lived several "turns" (*e.g.* the cultural or linguistic turn) and hence was nicknamed "the Latin America among sciences".

In the framework of the abovementioned course (Fig. **6**), students follow a track of:

- introduction into the motivation based on professional realities in developmental projects,
- resulting necessity of in-depth analyses of multiple standpoints starting from a learning platform, including studying the products of students in earlier semesters,
- authoring a personal standpoint discussing the requirements and bottlenecks of global development from the perspective of different world views and paradigms,
- following the in-class face-to-face lectures by the author in the traditional sense which build on the lecture slides but are not limited to it,
- writing peer reviews of two colleagues' standpoint papers mentioned above, following reflections during the lectures,
- as a facultative preparation for the final exam, writing six short documents on case studies regarding multicultural global development, out of 50 proposed themes,
- a final written exam, together with all other subject matters of the basic lecture (5 hours).

A full analysis of web-based student activities in the first year of GS was provided in [51] and can be summarised among others by diagnosing that by far the most web platform usage (90% of web hits and 95% of web time (Fig. **9**) was registered *after* the end of the traditional lectures. This finding underlines the capacity and *efficacy of technology-based scaffolding, especially by dialogue-oriented web platforms for multicultural learning*. Learning platforms are able to generate and support strong social and communicative dynamism among students which is consistent with a peer-oriented, discursive world view characteristic of modern democracies. By far the highest number of hits on a single page inside the learning platform was collected by a post containing comments on a peer review of a student standpoint which shows that "learning on a meta level", *i.e.* learning from how others see the *perspectives* of actors (not only the underlying facts) does come true in a suitable, technologically enhanced learning environment.

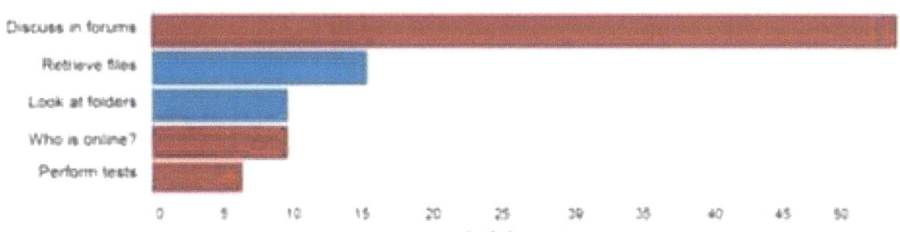

Fig. (9). Analysing the usage of tools by category shows that many more dialogic online tools such as discussion forums (red) are used than monologic online tools such as files or folders (blue).

Such experiences have given rise to the idea of inter-student activities being most crucial for the attainment of high academic quality. Peer interaction has inspired the concept of a jet principle.

In this paper, "jet principle" means that a dynamic process strongly relies on peer interaction of actors among themselves who behave in a self-responsible, autotelic, autopoietic [43] manner. Outer framework conditions only provide incentives to trigger and enhance such behaviour. Such a framework may be implemented by a web platform or by a system of rules defined for a course on how to reach a good mark or how to behave in game-based learning [52]. The jet turbine taken from engineering symbolises the discursive dynamics in multiparadigmatic learning. One of the core approaches of e-learning and learning technologies community is the view that technologies should be used to scaffold, *i.e.* facilitate learning [53].

In this text, development is understood as growing jointly in responsibility. The development of the notion of "development" [54]. is one of the most interesting and typical kaleidoscopes in development research, illustrating in a nutshell a series of quite controversial and antagonistic understandings of what pre-cognitive assumptions, tacit implications, logical consequences, strategic alliances and political strategies imply. Especially the entire volume of [55] highlight the conceptual development from endogenous theories (such as Rostow's five steps) to exogenous theories such as dependency theory (Frank, Prebisch), to Wallerstein's world-systems theory and further to post-development approaches such as Sen's capability approach in his "Development as Freedom" [56] or recent de-growth concepts. These developmental paradigms and their parallels in paradigms of history, sociology, geography and philosophy are discussed in [57] resulting in students' views) – but more thorough analysis is still necessary. In the face of the subjectivity of underlying concepts and their apparent speed of change, the author has chosen the above approach based on the spirit of responsibility, addressing approaches to human future, global system, institutions, ecology and social equity, in order to deliver a suitable working hypothesis for practice. These processes largely dwell on the notion of transdisciplinarity that is discussed in [58 - 62] and lead to proposing "Knowledge Alliances".

Kanbur [63] cites J.M. Keynes: "The ideas of economists and political philosophers, both when they are right and when they are wrong, are more powerful than is commonly understood. Indeed, the world is ruled by little else." This conviction forms one of the conceptual bases for analysis through "Global Studies".

Web based activities according to the "jet principle": Fig. (9) shows the aggregated web activities of students and highlights that there are mostly communication and discourse activities (dialogic: red) such as authoring review of papers and not mainly monologic activities blue) such as downloading texts in order to learn content.

Summary of the "Jet Principle" Process

The following Table 3 provides all details of the "jet principle" in a nutshell.

Table 3. Details of the teaching method "Jet Principle"

Title	The *"jet principle"* in e-learning
Overview of this teaching method	This form first defines the "jet principle" of (e-)learning as providing *dynamically suitable framework conditions* for enhanced learning procedures that interparadigmatically combine views from *multiple* cultures of science. *Social and learning procedures* proposed here are heuristically analysed based on 20 years of experience in interdisciplinary learning settings in a multicultural environment with a *critical approach to globalisation*, while also diverse scientific disciplines are counted as *"cultures of understanding"*. *Practical experiences* suggest that the application of this principle is capable of providing helpful framework conditions to multicultural learning that can suitably be applied in the *"Global Studies"* curriculum (*e.g.*, at universities in Graz, Salzburg, and Linz) as well as in other similar interdisciplinary curricula. *Quality criteria* are subject to scientific cultures and hence differ from discipline to discipline; thus representing a continuous challenge for a suitable perception of actors and bystanders. Complexities of cultural diversity are also reflected by complexities caused by the origins of diverse scientific cultures. In order to construct thorough and practically implementable consensus solutions, dialogic processes and peer review are best mediated through web-based discussion for which this paper provides examples. Discourse-oriented features and amendments for curricula of "Global Studies" are presented.

Self-Responsible Society   *Physics Education for Students: An Interdisciplinary Approach*   43

(Table 3) cont.....

Relation to sustainability:	As a result of considering different points of view (*e.g.* from construction companies and environmentalists), the arguments are discussed from the perspective of the divergent stakeholders. This creates social sustainability because negotiated solutions need not be renegotiated again. The other pillars of sustainability are incorporated herein by the lecturers' inputs and the students' individual research.
Group size	until 200 students.
Time required	1 semester.

Web Design for the "Jet Principle" in E-Learning

The following Fig. (**10**) provides visual impressions of a web-based implementation.

Fig. (10). Implementation of the "Jet Principle" at Graz University for students of Global Studies.

CONCLUSIONS

Experience of one decade of teaching showed that the two above-mentioned didactic procedures are capable of inciting students to higher levels of activity and consciousness, which pays off in increased levels of both factual understanding and societal engagement.

CONSENT FOR PUBLICATION

Not applicable.

CONFLICT OF INTEREST

The authors declare no conflict of interest, financial or otherwise.

ACKNOWLEDGEMENTS

Declared none.

REFERENCES

[1] M. Castells, *Identity and Change in the Network Society,* 20012012. http://globetrotter.berkeley.edu/people/Castells/castells-con0.html

[2] M. Czikszentmihalyi, *Flow: the psychology of optimal experience* Nightingale-Conant: New York, 1994.

[3] M. Handler, "Turning the Page - Future Dialogue 2035 (Das Blatt Wenden - Zukunftsdialog 2035)", *Austrian Society for Environment and Technology ÖGU,* 2010. http://www.dasblattwenden.at/english-summary/

[4] K. Kumpfmüller, Concordia versus Pax: The impact of Eastern governance for harmony on Western peace concepts.*Governance for harmony in Asia and beyond.,* J. Tao, A.B.L. Cheung, M. Painter, C. Li, Eds., Routledge: London, UK, 2009, pp. 329-334.

[5] M. Wolf, "Die vielsprachige Seele Kakaniens: Übersetzen und Dolmetschen in der Habsburgermonarchie 1848 bis 1918", *Böhlau, Vienna-Cologne-Weimar,* 2012.

[6] R. Galovic, "Energierevolution [Energy Revolution]", *Final Report from an Interdisciplinary Practical in Environmental Systems Sciences, USW Report SS,* Graz University, Austria, 2012. https://www.researchgate.net/publication/291496129_Energierevolution_Energy_Revolution

[7] K. Engelmann, "Energierevolution – Energieoptimierte Lebensweise und globaler Strukturwandel [Energy Revolution - energetically optimised way of life and global structural change]", *Final Report from an Interdisciplinary Practical in Environmental Systems Sciences, USW Report WS,* Graz University, Austria, 2012. https://www.researchgate.net/publication/291495429_Energierevolution_-_Energieoptimierte_Lebensweise_und_globaler_Strukturwandel_Energy_Revolution_-_energetically_optimised_way_of_life_and_global_structural_change

[8] A. Huskic, "Zukunftsdialog – Hat unsere Zukunft Zukunft? [Future Dialogue - Does our future have a future?]", *Final Report from an Interdisciplinary Practical in Environmental Systems Sciences, USW Report SS,* Graz University, Austria, 2011. https://www.researchgate.net/publication/291495350_Zukunftsdialog_-_Hat_unsere_Zukunft_Zukunft_Future_Dialogue_-_Does_our_future_have_a_future

[9] M. Buchsbaum, "Ökonomisch und ökologisch heizen – funktioniert das? Ein Vergleich verschiedener Heizungsmethoden [Heating ecologically and economically - does this work? A comparison of

different heating methods]", *Final Report from an Interdisciplinary Practical in Environmental Systems Sciences, USW Report SS,* Graz University, Austria, 2010. https://www.researchgate.net/publication/291486339_Okonomisch_und_okologisch_heizen_funktioniert_das_Ein_Vergleich_verschiedener_Heizungsmethoden_Heating_ecologically_and_economically_-_does_this_work_A_comparison_of_different_heating_methods

[10] V. Egger, "Die Ennsnahe Trasse: Jetzt oder Nie [The Highway along Enns river in Styria, Austria: now or never]", *Final Report from an Interdisciplinary Practical in Environmental Systems Sciences, USW Report WS,* Graz University, Austri, 2010. https://www.researchgate.net/publication/291486255_Die_Ennsnahe_Trasse_Jetzt_oder_Nie_The_Highway_along_Enns_river_in_Styria_Austria_now_or_never

[11] J. Baumgartner, "Ökologische Lebensweise [Ecological way of living]", *Final Report from an Interdisciplinary Practical in Environmental Systems Sciences, USW Report WS,* Graz University, Austria, 2009. https://www.researchgate.net/publication/291485570_Okologische_Lebensweise_Ecological_way_of_living

[12] G. Bachner, "Technologiefolgenabschätzung am Beispiel Klima [Technology Assessment - the example of climate change]", *Final Report from an Interdisciplinary Practical in Environmental Systems Sciences, USW Report SS,* Graz University, Austria, 2008. https://www.researchgate.net/publication/291476536_Technologiefolgenabschatzung_am_Beispiel_Klima_Technology_Assessment_-_the_example_of_climate_change

[13] S. Bauernhofer, "Energieoptimiertes Bauen und Wohnen [Constructing and living, energetically optimised]", *Final Report from an Interdisciplinary Practical in Environmental Systems Sciences, USW Report SS,* Graz University, Austria, 2008. https://www.researchgate.net/publication/291485554_Energieoptimiertes_Bauen_und_Wohnen_Constructing_and_living_energetically_optimised

[14] S. Adler, F. Augustin, T. Eder, C. Gruenwald, R. Holzer, G. Konrad, J. Kraxner, S. Kupsa, M. Pucher, M. Reiner, M. Sinwel, M. Sommer, J. Stangl, S. Teubl, D. Tudiwer, I. Wetz, G. Zahrer, S. Keeling, M. Mittelbach, and K. Steininger, "Peak Oil – Auswirkungen und Auswege für die Steiermark [Peak Oil – Effects and Escapes for Styria, Austria]", *Report number: USW Report,* Graz University, Austria, 2008. https://www.researchgate.net/publication/291357254_Peak_Oil_-_Auswirkungen_und_Auswege_fur_die_Steiermark_Peak_Oil_-_effects_and_escapes_for_Styria_Austria

[15] C. Enzi, "UVP und SUP - Nachhaltigkeitsbewertung in der Praxis [Environmental Impact Analysis (EIA) and Strategic Environmental Analysis (SEA) - sustainability assessment in practice]", *Final Report from an Interdisciplinary Practical in Environmental Systems Sciences, USW Report WS,* Graz University, Austria, 2008. https://www.researchgate.net/publication/291495897_UVP_und_SUP_-_Nachhaltigkeitsbewertung_in_der_Praxis_Environmental_Impact_Analysis_EIA_and_Strategic_Environmental_Analysis_SEA_-_sustainability_assessment_in_practice

[16] T. Baumhackl, "Globalisierung von Tschernobyl bis zur 380kV-Leitung [Globalisation from Chernobyl to the 380kV high voltage line in Styria, Austria]", *Final Report from an Interdisciplinary Practical in Environmental Systems Sciences, USW Report WS,* Graz University, Austria, 2008. https://www.researchgate.net/publication/291476492_Globalisierung_von_Tschernobyl_bis_zur_380kV-Leitung_Globalisation_from_Chernobyl_to_the_380kV_high_voltage_line_in_Styria_Austria

[17] S. Brunner, "Streitfall S7 - Pro und Contra des Projekts Fürstenfelder Schnellstraße [Case S7 - pros and cons of the highway project in Fürstenfeld, Styria, Austria]", *Final Report from an Interdisciplinary Practical in Environmental Systems Sciences, USW Report WS,* Graz University, Austria, 2008. https://www.researchgate.net/publication/291476025_Streitfall_S7_-_Pro_und_Contra_des_Projekts_Furstenfelder_Schnellstrasse_Case_S7_-_pros_and_cons_of_the_highway_project_in_Furstenfeld_Styria_Austria

[18] L.M. Erlandsen, "Ökologische Nachhaltigkeit am Beispiel Südosteuropa [Ecological Sustainability using the example of South-Eastern Europa]", *Final Report from an Interdisciplinary Practical in Environmental Systems Sciences, USW Report SS,* Graz University, Austria, 2007. https://www.researchgate.net/publication/291357228_Okologische_Nachhaltigkeit_am_Beispiel_Sudo

steuropa_Ecological_Sustainability_using_the_example_of_South-Eastern_Europa

[19] P. Anzenberger, "Zukunftsforschung - Zukünftige Wirtschaftsentwicklungen und deren Einfluss auf Gesellschaft und Natur [Future research - future economic developments and their influence on society and nature]", *Final Report from an Interdisciplinary Practical in Environmental Systems Sciences, USW Report SS,* Graz University, Austria, 2007. https://www.researchgate.net/publication/291357095_Zukunftsforschung_-_Zukunftige_Wirtschaftsentwicklungen_und_deren_Einfluss_auf_Gesellschaft_und_Natur_Future_research_-_future_economic_developments_and_their_influence_on_society_and_nature

[20] J. Albrecher, V. Aschauer, N. Baumgartner, K. Ebenschwaiger, S. Fischer, A. Fuchs, S. Greimel, F. Jarz, O. Konrad, C. Kozina, S. Lenz, C. Pacher, C. Pfeifer, J. Pichler, A. Plach, M. Schuller, M. Seidinger, T. Steiner, M. Sukitsch, and K. Schauer, "Ein Klima, um zu handeln [A climate to act]", *Final Report from an Interdisciplinary Practical in Environmental Systems Sciences, USW Report SS,* Graz University, Austria, 2007. https://www.researchgate.net/publication/291475753_Ein_Klima_um_zu_handeln_A_climate_to_act

[21] A. Schertler, "Passiv- und Niedrigenergiehaus [Passive houses and low-energy houses]", *Final Report from an Interdisciplinary Practical in Environmental Systems Sciences, USW Report SS,* Graz University, Austria, 2006. https://www.researchgate.net/publication/291355294_Passiv-_und_Niedrigenergiehaus_Passive_houses_and_low-energy_houses

[22] P. Arzberger, "Welt im Wandel? - Vergleich dreier sozioökonomischer, klimatischer & technologischer Zukunftsperspektiven [World in a Change - comparison of three socio-economic, climatic and technologic perspectives of the future]", *Final Report from an Interdisciplinary Practical in Environmental Systems Sciences, USW Report SS,* Graz University, Austria, 2005. https://www.researchgate.net/publication/291355104_Welt_im_Wandel_-_Vergleich_dreier_soziookonomischer_klimatischer_technologischer_Zukunftsperspektiven_World_in_a_Change_-_comparison_of_three_socio-economic_climatic_and_technologic_perspectives_of_th

[23] M. Damm, "Global Change - sozioökologische Kompetenzen am Beispiel der neuen EU-Mitgliedsstaaten [Global Change - socio-ecological competencies taking the example of the new EU member states]", *Final Report from an Interdisciplinary Practical in Environmental Systems Sciences, USW Report WS,* Graz University, Austria, 2005. https://www.researchgate.net/publication/291357239_Global_Change_-_soziookologische_Kompetenzen_am_Beispiel_der_neuen_EU-Mitgliedsstaaten_Global_Change_-_socio-ecological_competencies_taking_the_example_of_the_new_EU_member_states

[24] K. Maier, "Bürgerbeteiligung und Partizipation in der Nachhaltigkeitsplanung [Participation in sustainable planning]", *Final Report from an Interdisciplinary Practical in Environmental Systems Sciences, USW Report WS,* Graz University, Austria, 2005. https://www.researchgate.net/publication/291355004_Burgerbeteiligung_und_Partizipation_in_der_Nachhaltigkeitsplanung_Participation_in_sustainable_planning

[25] A. Biedermann, "Global Change in unserer vernetzten Welt [Global Change in our networked world]", *Final Report from an Interdisciplinary Practical in Environmental Systems Sciences, USW Report WS,* Graz University, Austria, 2004. https://www.researchgate.net/publication/291355043_Global_Change_in_unserer_vernetzten_Welt_Global_Change_in_our_networked_world

[26] W. Weiss, Solar Thermal Systems and Components.*Solar Heat Worldwide - Markets and Contribution to the Energy Supply 2009.* IEA Solar Heating & Cooling Programme, 2009. [http://dx.doi.org/10.18777/ieashc-shw-2009-0001]

[27] G. Ahamer, and C. Schrei, "Exercise 'Technology Assessment' through a gaming procedure", *J. Design Res.,* vol. 5, no. 2, pp. 224-252, 2006. [http://dx.doi.org/10.1504/JDR.2006.011364]

[28] G. Ahamer, and J. Mayer, "Forward looking: structural change and institutions in highest-income countries and globally", *Campus-Wide Inf. Syst.,* vol. 30, no. 5, pp. 386-403, 2013. [http://dx.doi.org/10.1108/CWIS-08-2013-0034]

[29] Dewey J., *Moral Principles in Education.* The Riverside Press: Cambridge, 1909.

[30] G. Ahamer, "Virtual Structures for mutual review promote understanding of opposed standpoints", *Turk. Online J. Dist. Educ.,* vol. 9, no. 1, pp. 17-43, 2008.

[31] R. Rorty, The Linguistic Turn. *Reprint.* University of Chicago Press, 1992.

[32] T. Tulku, *Time, Space, and Knowledge.* Dharma Publishing, 1977.

[33] K. Remele, *Ziviler Ungehorsam: eine Untersuchung aus der Sicht christlicher Sozialethik.* Habilitation, Aschendorff Verlag: Münster, 1992.

[34] G. Ahamer, "The jet principle: technologies provide border conditions for global learning", *Multicul. Educ. Techn. J,* vol. 6, no. 3, pp. 177-210, 2012.

[35] G. Ahamer, "A four-dimensional Maxwell equation for social processes in web-based learning and teaching – windrose dynamics as GIS: games' intrinsic spaces", *Int. J. Web-Based Learn. Teach. Technol.,* vol. 7, no. 3, pp. 1-19, 2012.
[http://dx.doi.org/10.4018/jwltt.2012070101]

[36] J. Rau, "The Nagorno-Karabakh Conflict between Armenia and Azerbaijan", *A Brief Historical Outline,* Verlag Dr. Köster: Berlin, 20082012. http://www.verlag-koester.de/buch.php?id=592&fb_id=49

[37] Y.-F Chang, and E. Liu, "Investigating Adolescent Bloggers from the Perspective of Creative Subculture", *Intern. J. Online Ped. Course Design,* vol. 1, no. 1, pp. 31-45, 2011.

[38] T. Huseynov, *A Moment of Truth in the Nagorno-Karabakh Talks?,* 20102012. http://www.crisisgroup.org/en/regions/europe/south-caucasus/azerbaijan/huseynov-a-moment-of-truth-in-the-nagorno-karabakh-talks.aspx

[39] G. Ahamer, K.A. Kumpfmüller, and H. Hohenwarter, "Web-based exchange of views enhances 'Global Studies'", *Campus-Wide Inf. Syst.,* vol. 28, no. 1, pp. 16-40, 2011.
[http://dx.doi.org/10.1108/10650741111097278]

[40] Exl, *Principle of a jet turbine,* 2006. http://www.exl.at/helicopter/turbinen/turbinen.htm http://www.grc.nasa.gov/WWW/K-12/airplane/ngnsim.html

[41] Dorst, and I. Reymen, "Levels of Expertise in Design Education", *International Engineering and Product Design Education Conference, Delft,* 20042012. http://doc.utwente.nl/58083/1/levels_of_expertise.pdf

[42] J. Restrepo, and H. Christiaans, "Problem Structuring and Information Access in Design", *J. Design Res.,* vol. 4, no. 2, 2004.
[http://dx.doi.org/10.1504/JDR.2004.009842]

[43] J.D. Sterman, *Business Dynamics: Systems thinking and modelling for a complex world.* McGraw-Hill: Boston, 2000.

[44] BBC, *Regions and territories: Nagorno-Karabakh,* 2010. http://news.bbc.co.uk/2/hi/europe/country_profiles/3658938.stm

[45] Global Security, *The Nagorno-Karabakh conflict,* 2010. http://www.globalsecurity.org/military/world/war/nagorno-karabakh-1.htm

[46] H. Gebhardt, R. Glaser, U. Radtke, P. Reuber, and P. Geography,

[47] H. Lefebvre, *The Production of Space.* Wiley-Blackwell: Oxford, 1992.

[48] E.W. Soja, *Postmodern Geographies: The Reassertion of Space in Critical Social Theory.* Verso: London, 2011.

[49] D. Harvey, *The Condition of Postmodernity: An Enquiry into the Origins of Cultural Change.* Wiley-Blackwell: Oxford, 1991.

[50] K.W. Rothschild, "Economics as a multiparadigmatic science", *Conference in Honour of Kurt W. Rothschild (1914-2010), Vienna,* 20112012. http://www.kurt-rothschild.at/konferenz2011.php

[51] G. Ahamer, "How Technologies Can Localize Learners in Multicultural Space: A Newly Developed "Global Studies" Curriculum", *Marketing Strategies for Higher Education Institutions: Technological Considerations and Practices.,* pp. 103-127, 2013.*IGI Global, Hershey, PA: Business Science Reference,* pp. 103-127, 2013.

[52] S. Naidu, A. Ip, and R. Linser, "Dynamic goal-based role-play simulation on the web: a case study", *J. Educ. Technol. Soc.,* vol. 3, no. 3, pp. 190-202, 2000.

[53] M. Prensky, *Digital game-based learning.* McGraw Hill: Boston, 2001.

[54] R. Kanbur, The Development of Development Thinking, *Lecture delivered at the Institute for Social and Economic Change,* Bangalore during tenure as V.K.R.V. Rao Chair Professor at the Institute.: Cornell University, 20052012. http://www.arts.cornell.edu/poverty/kanbur/ISECLecture.pdf

[55] "Klassiker der Entwicklungstheorie – Von Modernisierung bis Post-Development of the series Gesellschaft - Entwicklung - Politik (GEP = society - development – policy)", *Wien, Mandelbaum,* vol. 11, 2008.

[56] A. Sen, *Development as Freedom.* Oxford University Press: Oxford, 1999.

[57] G. Ahamer, GIS^S and GIS^P facilitate higher education and cooperative learning design. *Handbook of Research on Transnational Higher Education Management.,* S. Mukerji, P. Tripathi, Eds., vol. I. IGI Global Publishers: USA, 2013, pp. 1-21.

[58] S. Howorka, and S. Kultur, "Kultur und Interkulturalität im transdisziplinären Forschungsprojekt „Ungleiche Vielfalt", *Contribution to the Workshop Interkulturalität als Instrumentarium für Einsatz und Führung,* Paolo-Freire Centre: Vienna, 2012.

[59] M. Stigendal, "Elipse – European to Local Innovation for best Practice policy development com¬bating Social Exclusion", *final report, Malmö Univ,* 20032012. http://ezone.mah.se/projects/

[60] M. Stigendal, "Intercultural competence among young people in deprived neighbourhoods", *Workshop on Intercultural competence,* 2009 Malmö

[61] M. Stigendal, "Cities and Social Cohesion", *Popularizing the results of Social Polis,* Publications in Urban Studies (MAPIUS) 6: Malmö University, 20102012. http://www.mikaelstigendal.se

[62] M. Stigendal, "Founding knowledge alliances", *Unpublished manuscript,* Malmö University, 2012. http://wpmu.mah.se/lumist/in-english/

[63] R. Kanbur, "The Development of Development Thinking", *Lecture delivered at the Institute for Social and Economic Change,* Bangalore during tenure as V.K.R.V. Rao Chair Professor at the Institute: Cornell University, 20052012. http://www.arts.cornell.edu/poverty/kanbur/ISECLecture.pdf

CHAPTER 4

Dialogic Best Practice for Dissemination of A Scientific Culture

Gilbert Ahamer[1,*]

[1] *Karl-Franzens University Graz, Institute for Economic and Social History, Universitätsstrasse 15/F2, 8010 Graz, Austria*

Abstract: In the face of globalization, the question arises which didactic and educational strategy based on self-responsibility is best suited for dissemination of a science-based humanitarian culture.

This chapter reflects one pedagogic approach to strengthen self-responsibility within students, namely the approach "Surfing Global Change" (SGC,© G. Ahamer) which relies on dialogue while confronting learners with their peers – a much-needed training event when it comes to real-live professional situations.

This article portrays the 5-level rule structure and offers graphic implementation and moreover some results on emerging social dynamics within student groups.

This method is suitable for advanced physics students in any transdisciplinary setting.

Keywords: Curriculum, Dialogic learning, Discursive learning, Globalization, Global studies, Global Studies Consortium, Graz University, Interparadigmatic, Quality assurance, Transdisciplinary.

SURFING GLOBAL CHANGE

Pedagogic Foundation of the Negotiation Game "Surfing Global Change"

The pedagogic goal of this negotiation game SGC (© G. Ahamer) is to teach students how to take on a proactive and technically responsible role for sustainably building a global society. Didactic and pedagogical principles are described in detail in the published literature [1]. This succinct overview presents the SGC rules in the typically used graphic design of SGC.

---

[*] **Corresponding author Gilbert Ahamer:** Karl-Franzens University Graz, Institute for Economic and Social History, Universitätsstrasse 15/F2, 8010 Graz, Austria; E-mail: gilbert.ahamer@uni-graz.at

Maria Teresa Caccamò and Salvatore Magazù (Eds.)
All rights reserved-© 2021 Bentham Science Publishers

This entire 5-level game "Surfing Global Change" has the learning objective to master consensus building as practiced and demanded in many developed societies [2, 3].

In more detail this means five levels [4, 5] (compare Fig. **1**). At the same time, the following figures inform about the graphic design which was developed for SGC by the information graphics expert Chris Schrei in Graz (www.definite.at).

GAME OVERVIEW

Fig. (1). The levels of the entire game SGC (© G. Ahamer) are founded on each other. These lead to greater social and academic complexity and enhance suitability of the constructed consensus.

The didactic goals are further identified in Fig. (**2**).

Fig. (**2**). The five social actions are based on the didactic goals of SGC [6].

As a result of didactic approaches, (Fig. **3**) provides the game approach of SGC.

Fig. (3). SGC's game approach, using five levels of rising social complexity [7].

The social procedures server to practically implement the didactic vision (Fig. **4**).

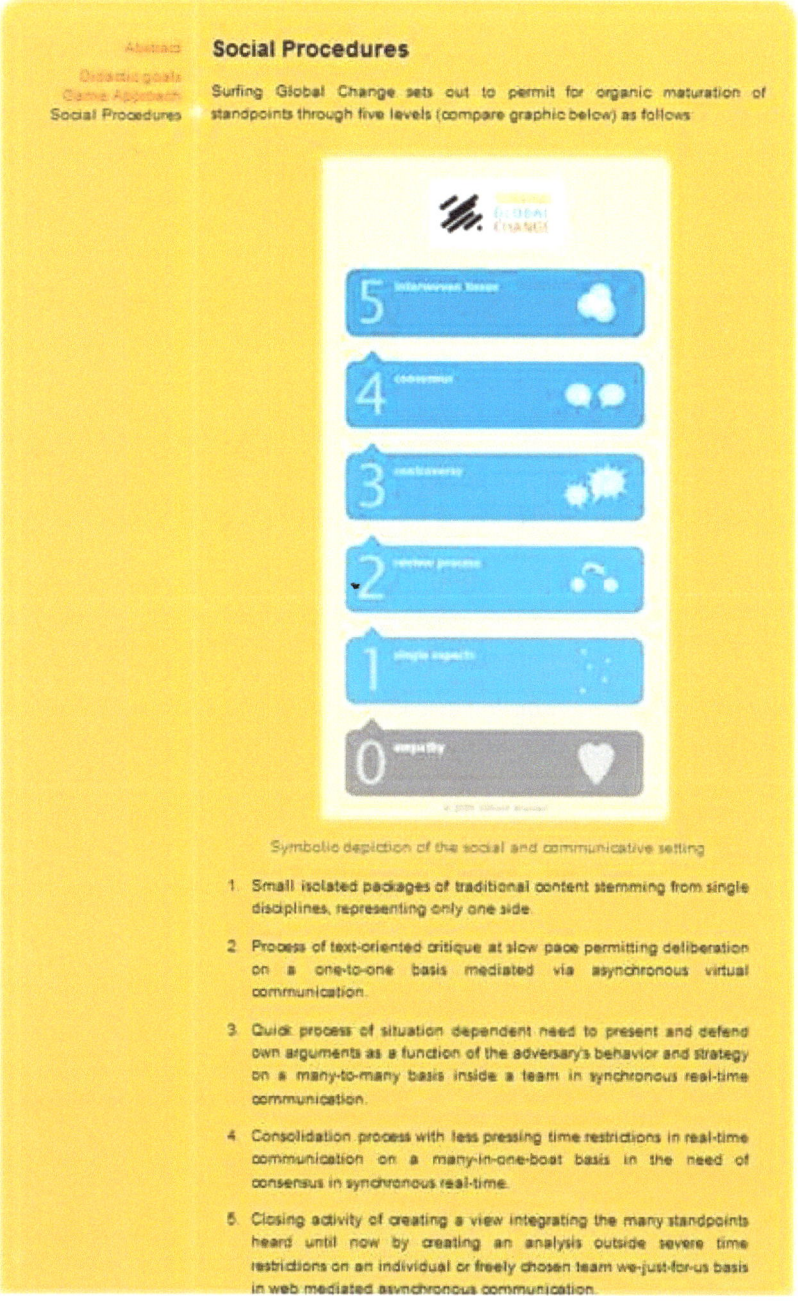

Fig. (4). Social procedures in SGC, according to the five levels of rising social complexity [8].

Interdisciplinarity

The *bridge across selective perceptions* since long denotes the need that students tend to acquire knowledge starting from the scientific home discipline they originally learned: the ecologist will think of nuclear waste and so-called "Negawatts" (= not using electric energy) while an engineer continues to think of Megawatts, quite classically. The situation of a real-life solution for multi-stakeholder issues requires to perceive

- economic rationality
- technological feasibility
- environmental and social equilibriums

with the target to satisfying needs for perseverating (*i.e.*, "sustainably lasting") acceptance by all populations. The "Green Deal" and the "Environmental Impact Assessment Directive" in EU legislation implemented this thinking that already led to a set of clear administrative procedures for a large-scale infrastructural project.

A Variety of Value Systems: Becoming Interparadigmatic

Perceiving and taking into account diverse "ethical measurement systems" is a skill to highly important for the global labour market, for all in countries affected by migration, with multi-ethnic or with multi-religious backgrounds. To participate is a mode of life to incorporate various stakeholders' systemic values during every planning procedure [6].

The above considerations show that consistent and contemporary education should foster skills to build bridges between:

1. different lenses by which stakeholders perceive and assess issues
2. different patterns or stakeholders' cultures of understanding
3. different stakeholders' metrics by which suitability of solutions are judged.

When we take into account (a) re-framing along learners' paths for enhancing learning and (b) switching between roles assumed for learning encouragement, an optimally designed role play [7] promises good results and strengthens authentic entrepreneurship [8]. The negotiation game SGC locates learners repeatedly within situations exhibiting ever increasing academic and social complexity.

The author suggests "include learners *via* procedural learning innovation" in order to include the above-mentioned three challenges.

THE RULES FOR THE GAME "SURFING GLOBAL CHANGE"

Experience has shown for physics curricula or for interdisciplinary curricula that it is advisable to first acquire sufficient levels of knowledge [9 - 14], before walking through a more elaborated didactic program (level 1 in Fig. **3**).

While Fig. (**5**) showed the introductory level 0, Fig. (**6**) shows a content-oriented level 1.

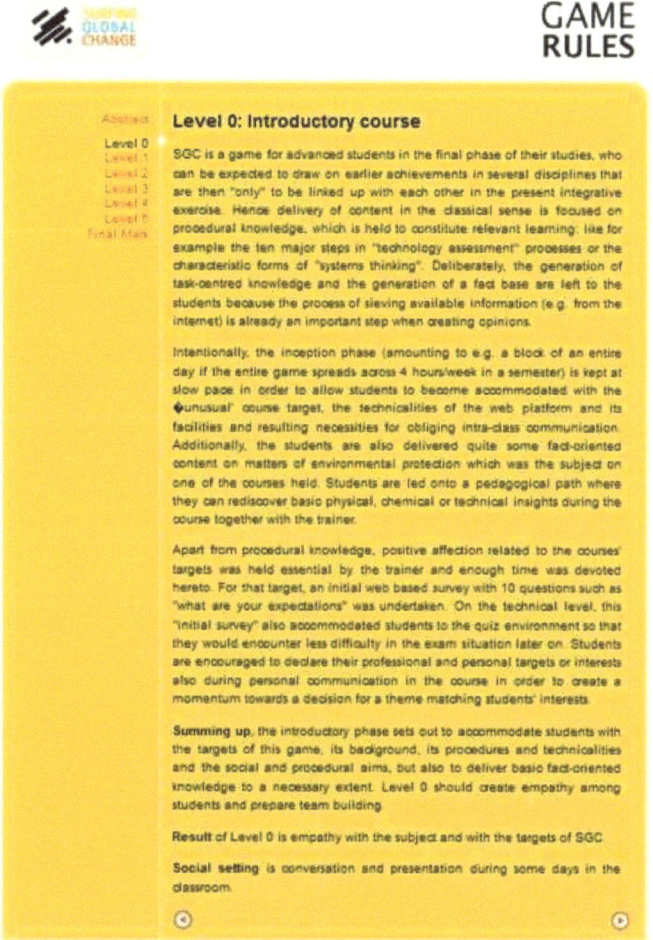

Fig. (5). SGC level 0 provides an introductory course [15, 16], creating empathy with and among learners.

Level 1: Understand content and sharpen target

During the subsequent Level 1 (or if necessary also a second time later on), a web based quiz is held during class that plays the role of a traditional written exam.

$$(\text{success in web based quiz}) = \text{points } \underline{\varepsilon}$$

Points collected there contribute roughly one third to the final mark of the individual students. Questions are formulated in a way to exclude mere reproduction of pieces of text which serves as a means to decrease probability of cheating.

A rather simple and common interactive game serves to sharpen perception of the factual setting of the task: a modified "8-4-2 words" game (similar to the Delphi method) should help students to further focus on the target of the game. Three questions for definitions are posed, e.g. concerning course's content and perspective (♦'Global Change', consensus'), a target, aim or other central notion (e.g. ♦'sustainability') and the chosen theme (e.g. a railway tunnel project, mobile phone antennas) are elaborated iteratively in the following way using the web platform:

- Each student anonymously posts an answer in 8 words during class.
- All students are presented the answers (= definitions) anonymously and cast a vote for the best one including a short sentence of explaining their decision.
- The statistical result is displayed by the trainer together with the (anonymous) total of explanations in order to allow for a learning effect.
- For each posting or voting action a student receives one point from the trainer.
- The same procedure as above starts with 4 words, then with 2 words.
- Aim: Viewing other colleagues' answers allows for rethinking the own perception in an undisturbed and private atmosphere without outer social pressure.

$$(\text{each posting or voting in the web platform for the 8-4-2 game}) = 1 \text{ point } \underline{\varepsilon}$$

The set of game rules acts as a boundary condition for expected processes of social self-organization. Interest for a good mark (resulting from collected rewards) steers team size, work attitude and individuals' affinity to sticking to own convictions when substantiating consensus. SGC's rules trigger two distinct processes: social dynamics among peer students in the class and their individual strive for marks for the course. These two targets provide useful tension during game play.

Summing up, Level 1 should incite students to discern and define their area

Fig. (6). SGC level 1 provides basic and advanced knowledge [17 - 19] to learners.

Level 2 (Fig. **7**) models a peer review process while Figs. (**8** - **11**) model a multi-actor negotiation situation as in Environmental Impact Assessment (EIA).

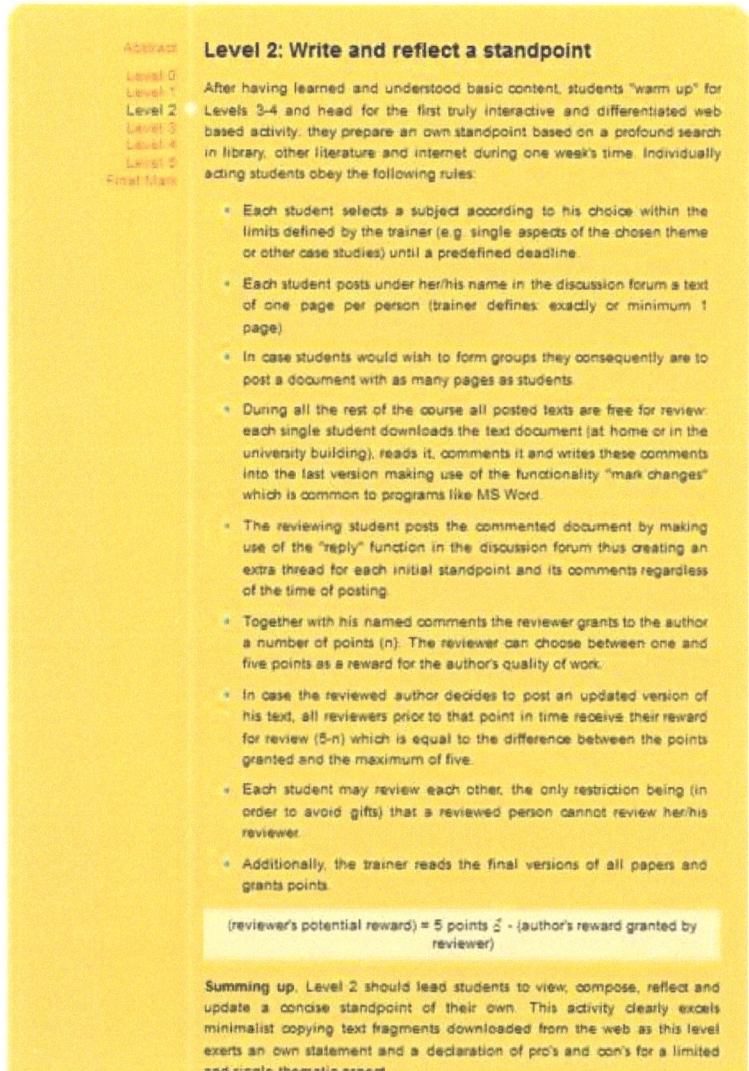

Fig. (7). SGC level 2 allows learners to engage in a 1:1 author-reviewer relationship.

Level 3: Weigh aspects of a theme

After having decided on two (one half of class is discussing, the other half observing) concrete themes for Levels 3 and 4 and after the decision for a suitable matrix either by the students or the trainer the following guidelines apply:

- The students decide which role (which type of actor) they want to take as a team inside the chosen theme, e.g.
  - proponent of the (building) project
  - civil authority deciding on the permission to implement this project (e.g. by means of an environmental impact assessment procedure EIA)
  - lobby of economy and industry
  - lobby of the environmentalists

- The generation of teams is governed by the formula

  (reviewer's potential reward) = 5 points ξ - (author's reward granted by reviewer)

  therefore the team size is expected to be optimized between very small (not enough manpower) and very large (too little share of reward) team size.

- Each team has one team speaker to communicate decisions externally.
- Only the team speaker is named to the trainer, the process of team generation, constitution and definition of internal roles is left to the students.
- Team leaders have the right to expulse members (e.g. if not collaborating)
- The students have one week of time for preparing common and agreed standpoints in teams (2 pages per person) on the theme that was agreed on beforehand.
- After one week the (mostly four) teams are to post their standpoint in form of a consistent and outweighed document into the web platform.
- On the day of the Level 3 game, all single teams are asked to sit at their tables in the center of the class room (inner part of graphic below) and they are given a piece of paper with the matrix (e.g. 3x4, showing headings for rows and columns as well as definitions for each matrix square).

Fig. (8a). SGC level 3 models a multi-party negotiation [20] in a competitive n:n relationship.

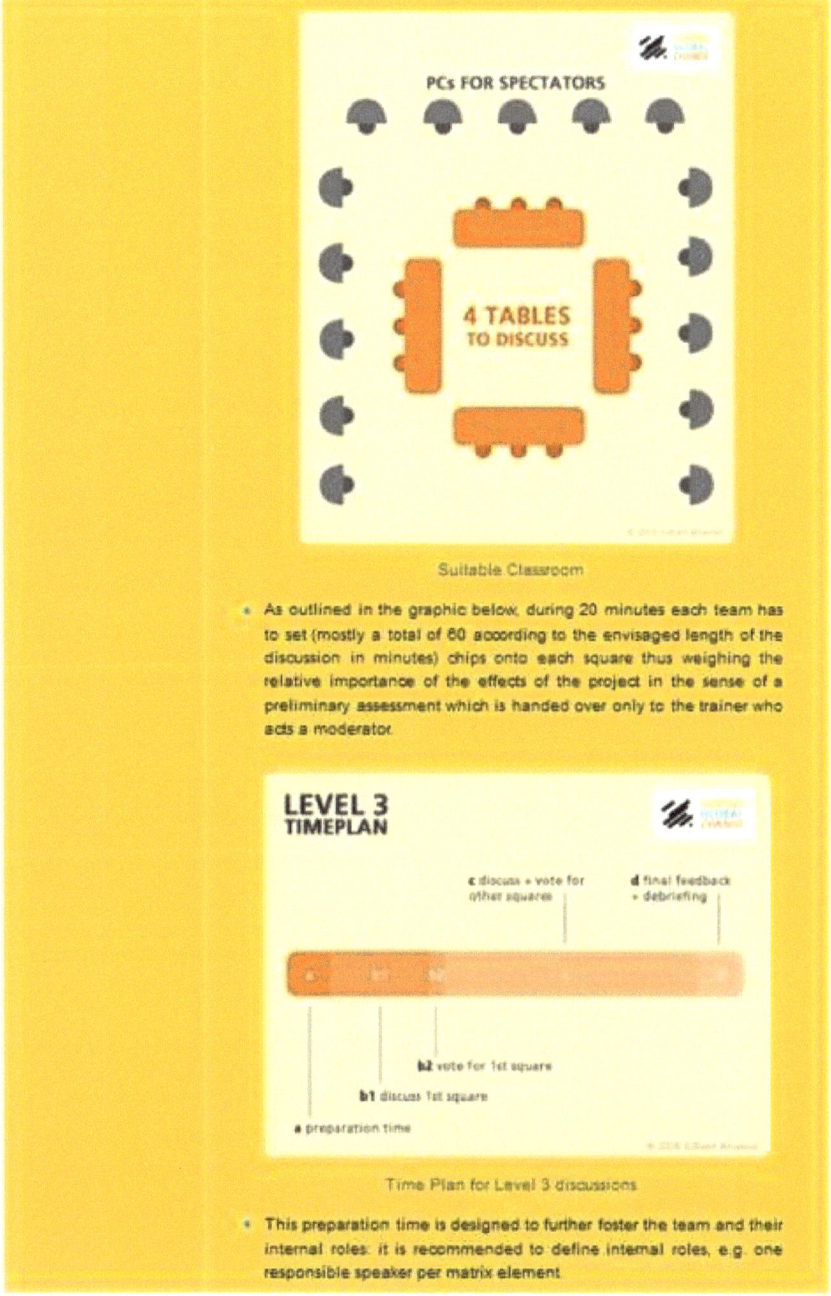

Fig. (8b). SGC level 3 models a multi-party negotiation in a competitive n:n relationship.

new university campus	economic	environmental	infrastructure	landscape	social
city population and neighbors		20			
students			5		2
business people	1				
university operators	15				5
city council			10	5	

- During discussions the trainer (or supporting software) randomly selects one matrix square after the other to learn, which teams have set chips.
- Only teams having set chips discuss on the respective subject obeying the rule for the discussion time (if appropriate with 10 min. as a minimum).

(time in minutes) = (sum of chips set on the square) / (number of involved teams)

- The remaining teams at tables not having set chips plus the students belonging to the other theme (spectators outer part of the classroom graphic) form the public with a right to vote (e.g. directly or also via the platform).
- Optionally a jury (e.g. of external experts or selected students or the trainer her/himself) is present in the room.
- The trainer marks start and end of the discussion (e.g. with an alarm clock or web software), but refrains from participation in the content or procedure.
- After the end of discussion the "public" has the following options for voting:
    - Each single participating team has won the discussion
    - A substantial consensus was reached among the teams
    - No team has won the discussion (e.g. only seemingly a consensus)
- In case (1) only the winning team receives the reward according to the following formula, in case (2) all involved teams, in case (3) no team.

(time in minutes) = (sum of chips set on the square) / (number of involved teams)

- The voting jury is obliged to give a reason for their decision, the voting public may, but need not do so and receives 1 point for each posted reason.

Fig. (8c). SGC level 3 models a multi-party negotiation in a competitive n:n relationship.

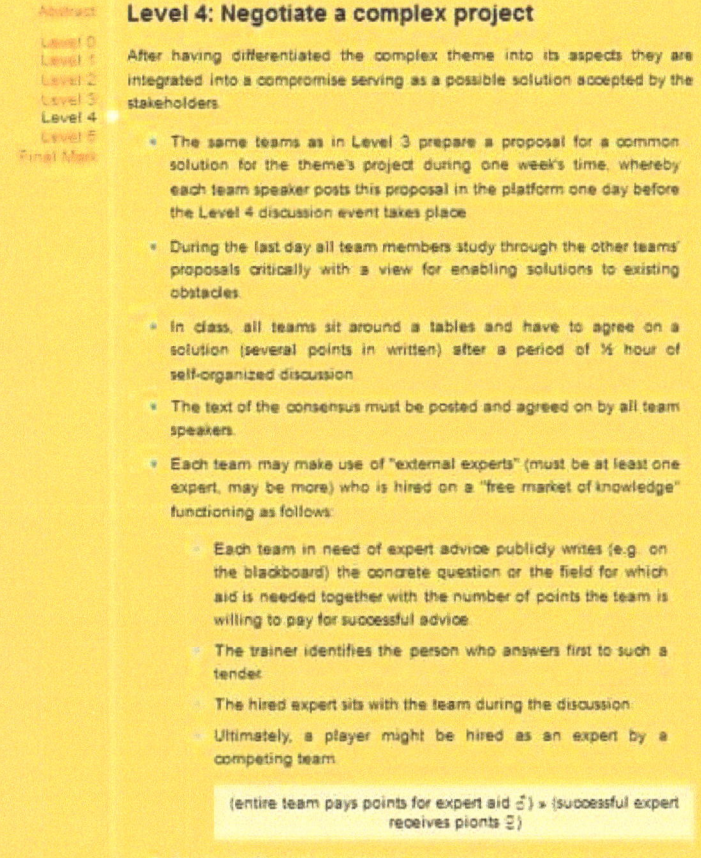

Fig. (9). SGC level 4 offers a consensus-oriented multi-party negotiation setting.

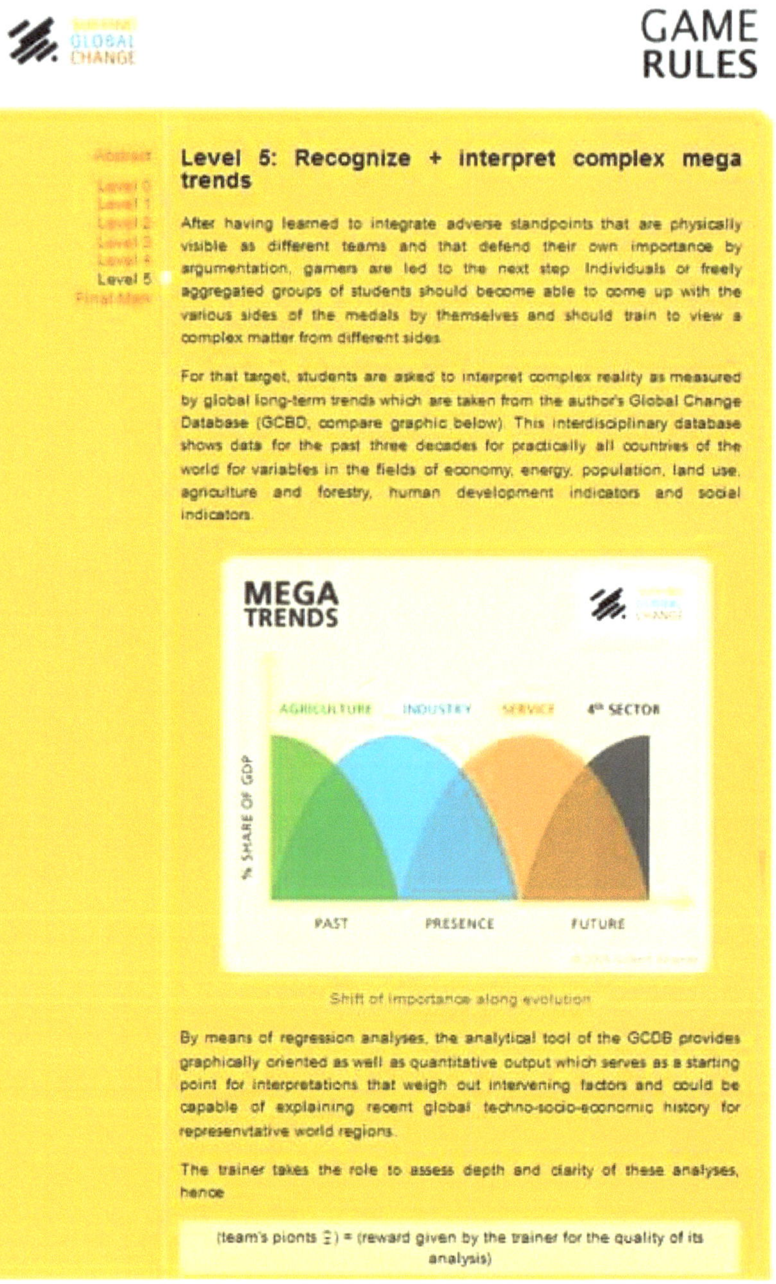

Level 5: Recognize + interpret complex mega trends

After having learned to integrate adverse standpoints that are physically visible as different teams and that defend their own importance by argumentation, gamers are led to the next step. Individuals or freely aggregated groups of students should become able to come up with the various sides of the medals by themselves and should train to view a complex matter from different sides.

For that target, students are asked to interpret complex reality as measured by global long-term trends which are taken from the author's Global Change Database (GCBD, compare graphic below). This interdisciplinary database shows data for practically the past three decades for practically all countries of the world for variables in the fields of economy, energy, population, land use, agriculture and forestry, human development indicators and social indicators.

MEGA TRENDS

AGRICULTURE   INDUSTRY   SERVICE   4th SECTOR

% SHARE OF GDP

PAST   PRESENCE   FUTURE

Shift of importance along evolution

By means of regression analyses, the analytical tool of the GCDB provides graphically oriented as well as quantitative output which serves as a starting point for interpretations that weigh out intervening factors and could be capable of explaining recent global techno-socio-economic history for representative world regions.

The trainer takes the role to assess depth and clarity of these analyses, hence

(team's pionts ≑) = (reward given by the trainer for the quality of its analysis)

Fig. (10). SGC level 5 encourages to frame the learned complexities [21, 22] within global long-term trends.

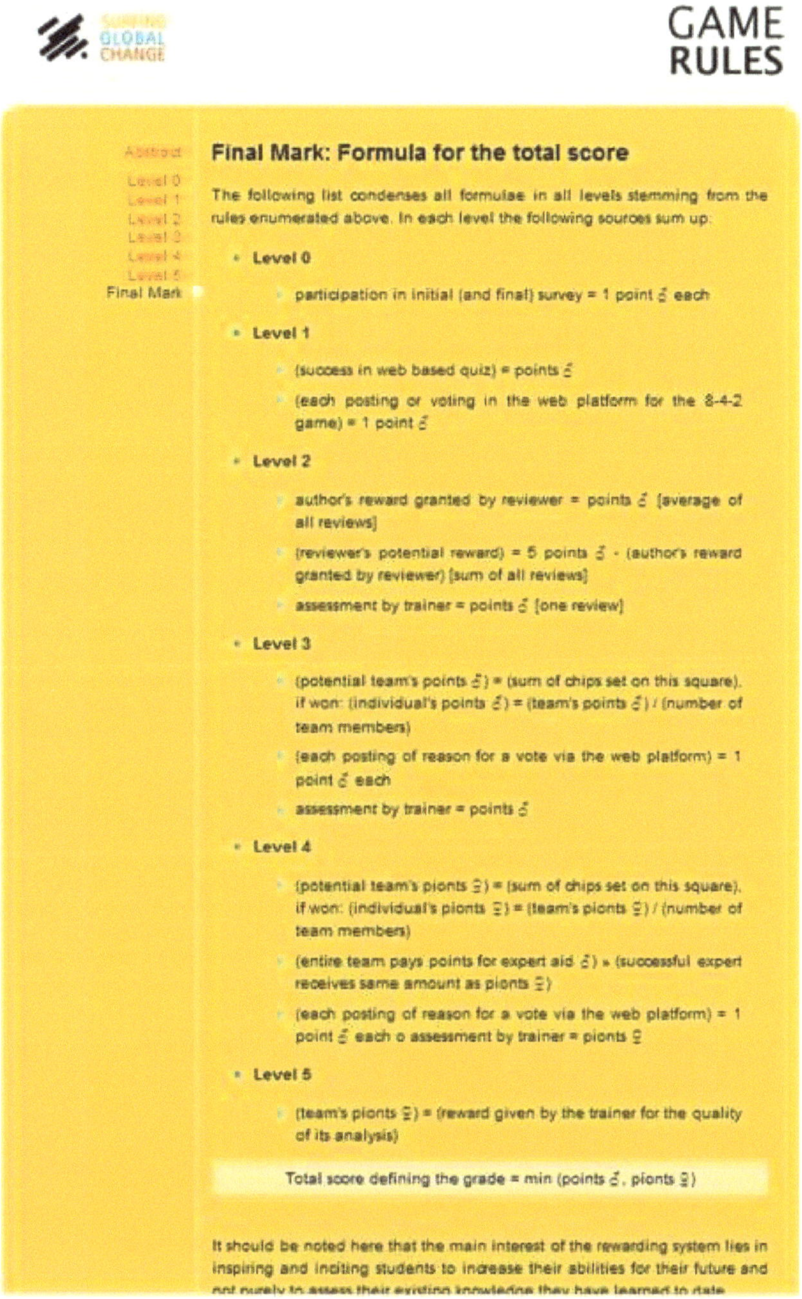

Scientific Culture   *Physics Education for Students: An Interdisciplinary Approach*   63

Final Mark: Formula for the total score

The following list condenses all formulae in all levels stemming from the rules enumerated above. In each level the following sources sum up:

- **Level 0**
  - participation in initial (and final) survey = 1 point $\eth$ each

- **Level 1**
  - (success in web based quiz) = points $\eth$
  - (each posting or voting in the web platform for the 8-4-2 game) = 1 point $\eth$

- **Level 2**
  - author's reward granted by reviewer = points $\eth$ [average of all reviews]
  - (reviewer's potential reward) = 5 points $\eth$ - (author's reward granted by reviewer) [sum of all reviews]
  - assessment by trainer = points $\eth$ [one review]

- **Level 3**
  - (potential team's points $\eth$) = (sum of chips set on this square), if won: (individual's points $\eth$) = (team's points $\eth$) / (number of team members)
  - (each posting of reason for a vote via the web platform) = 1 point $\eth$ each
  - assessment by trainer = points $\eth$

- **Level 4**
  - (potential team's pionts $\female$) = (sum of chips set on this square), if won: (individual's pionts $\female$) = (team's pionts $\female$) / (number of team members)
  - (entire team pays points for expert aid $\eth$) = (successful expert receives same amount as pionts $\female$)
  - (each posting of reason for a vote via the web platform) = 1 point $\eth$ each o assessment by trainer = pionts $\female$

- **Level 5**
  - (team's pionts $\female$) = (reward given by the trainer for the quality of its analysis)

Total score defining the grade = min (points $\eth$, pionts $\female$)

It should be noted here that the main interest of the rewarding system lies in inspiring and inciting students to increase their abilities for their future and not purely to assess their existing knowledge they have learned to date.

Fig. (11). The final marks for students are computed as the sum from all levels' point achieved.

OVERVIEW OF THE GAME "SURFING GLOBAL CHANGE"

Table 1. Overview of Surfing Global Change (SGC).

Title	Surfing Global Change (SGC), © Gilbert Ahamer
Overview of this teaching method	"**Surfing Global Change**" (SGC) is a didactically sound and innovative online-based course in 5 levels for variable interdisciplinary courses. The attractiveness of SGC results from the didactic approach ("discourse ethics"), and SGC was recognized by the British scientific publisher Emerald with the "Outstanding Paper Award 2005". SGC's appeal is based on the didactic approach ("ethics of discourse"). SGC's special feature is the abandonment of "absolute truths" (which would have to be learned) in favour of **achieving negotiated solutions** with the objective of sustainable and lasting consensus solutions between the role-playing participants. SGC is process-oriented training for the intricacies of professional careers [23 - 25] because it focuses on structural conflicts of interest. What is special about SGC is the abandonment of "truths in themselves" (which would have to be learned) in favour of reaching negotiated solutions with the aim of achieving lasting consensus between the role-playing participants. SGC trains process-oriented for the depths of professional life because it prepares conflicts of interest. The focus is on gradually becoming more complex, rhythmic social processes among the participants who, in changing team compositions, research technical fundamentals from the perspectives of different actors, comprehend them in writing, review each other, try to enforce them in controversial debates, weigh them up in consensual conferences and finally put in the broad context of global megatrends. The usability of SGC was improved from the basis in 2005. Its basis is "blended learning", therefore SGC is not about virtual gimmicks, but addresses the needs of well cooperating students (often over 1000 hits / semester per student), who find course materials and express their expectations in surveys, discuss to achieve points, perform tests [26 - 30] and engage in review processes.

(Table 1) cont.....

Title	Surfing Global Change (SGC), © Gilbert Ahamer

Main description text	<u>Learning scenario</u>: The emerging social dynamics is generated by a detailed set of rules (see bibliography), which is available online in the "game rules" (shown on 1 page each per level).
	<u>Method</u>: The five-step negotiation "Surfing Global Change" **trains the *skills for achieving sustainable consensus solutions***. Along a series of game processes in five levels (Fig. 1, right) the share of social skills increases as compared to classical professional skills:
	    1. *Level 1:* acquiring knowledge and pass a web-based quiz
	    2. *Level 2:* establishing a sound technical point of view and comment on others' views
	    3. *Level 3:* winning a controversial discussion in the team in the view of observers
	    4. *Level 4:* reaching consensus with the same discussion partners
	    5. *Level 5:* integrating the envisaged case study in the context of global long-term trends.
	The <u>goal</u> of Surfing Global Change is to construct your own learning goals, to increase the transdisciplinary competence of the game participants in order to generate long-lasting (sustainable) solutions in the face of conflicting patterns of interest. Technical, economic, social and other effects of large projects or innovations [31 - 33] can be systematically assessed and compared against values ("**technology assessment**").
	<u>Aim</u>: SGC radically promotes the **emergence of dynamic inter-students communication patterns**. This – as in real life – may be dominated by the pursuit of self-interest as well as by the commitment to professional quality. In this **area of tension**, a sensitive and often deliberately unstable social equilibrium builds up, in which the students can experience first-hand the imponderables of both Machiavellian and idealistic behaviour based on their own behavioural tendencies. The moderator accompanies and supports.
	The <u>role of the evaluator</u> is largely transferred from the moderator to the students. These themselves define case studies, teams, points of view and strategies and give themselves points (for the grade).
	The concept of this learning suite has been implemented at a university and a technical college since 2003 and has so far been implemented several dozen times in the following courses:
	    1. "*Technology Assessment*", "*Environmental Technology*", "*Systems Theory & Biology*" in the curricula "Civil Engineering", "Architecture" and "Industrial Electronics" at FH Joanneum
	    2. "*Interdisciplinary Practicals*" in the curriculum "Environmental Systems Sciences" of the University of Graz on the themes
	        o *Technology Assessment*
	        o *Climate Change and Climate Models*
	        o *Systems Analysis and Biology*
	        o *Global Change – Socio-ecologic competencies considering for example the new EU Member States*
	        o *Environmental effects of land use and energy supply*
	        o *Global Change in our networked environment*
	        o *Participation in Municipal Sustainability Planning*
	        o *Passive Houses and Low Energy Houses*
	        o *World in a Change? - Comparison of three socio-economic, climatic and technological future perspectives*
	        o *A Climate to Act*
	        o *Environment in South-East Europe and EU Enlargement*
	        o *Futurology*
	        o *Peak Oil*
	        o *Energy Optimization in the Residential Sector*
	        o *Technology Assessment and Climate Change*
	        o *S7 - Pro and Contra of the Fürstenfeld Highway*
	        o *EIA & Strategic Environmental Assessment SEA*
	        o *Ecological Way of Life: Nostalgic Past or Necessary Future?*
	        o *Globalization from Chernobyl to the Styrian 380kV line*
	        o *Go East: Environmental Aspects in Croatia and Slovenia*
	        o *Viticulture in Southern Styria under Impact of Climate Chg.*
	        o *Heating Ecologically and Economically: Comparing Methods*
	        o *Inner-Alpine Highway along the Enns River: Now or Never*
	    3. Seminar "Globalisation & Global Change" at Salzburg Univ.

(Table 1) cont.....

Title	Surfing Global Change (SGC), © Gilbert Ahamer
Educational objective/learning outcomes:	• Understand complex interdisciplinary issues that include several, often antagonistic actors/stakeholders • Understand your counterparts in international projects
Group size	10 – 20 students. Also, larger groups possible
Time required	1 semester. The SGC processes use up around one weekly hour for a semester. Other such hours are recommended for fact-oriented lectures.

BASICS OF WEB DESIGN FOR SGC

Building on the above "**Rules for SGC**" (level 0: (Fig. **5**); level 1: (Fig. **6**); level 2: (Fig. **7**); level 3: (Fig. **8**); level 4: (Fig. **9**); and level 5: (Fig. **10**)) and the referenced literature describing the choice for the didactic functionality and background of SGC, this subchapter illustrates the structure of a suitable structure on conventional web-based learning platforms (Figs. **12** and **13**). Analogue structures can be built on other web platforms that may be different from the Canadian product WebCT (Web Course Tools) displayed in this chapter here.

Fig. (12). Welcome web sites for SGC.

Fig. (13). Internal web sites for SGC.

CONCLUSIONS

For the mentioned integrated pedagogical aims, a suite of concrete didactic procedures was proposed for usage in higher education: the web-supported negotiation game SGC ("**Surfing Global Change**", © G. Ahamer) enables and enhances a process of achieving a holistic view on complex intercultural and interdisciplinary realities including divergent stakeholders' value systems. SGC uses a game-based learning tradition through employing problem-based, situated learning strategies, additionally enhanced by synchronous and asynchronous www-based interaction.

The present chapter illustrated the official set of game rules of this original game invented, implemented and copyrighted by the author at the turn of the millennium.

SGC's didactics is grounded in self-organized, active, *self-directed learning*, training of the empowerment to act and for self-motivated responsibility towards both sustainable and practicable solutions for our future planetary society.

The pedagogic outlay of SGC aims at equlilibrating consensus *vs.* competition, team work *vs.* self-study, readiness to compromise *vs.* sharpening one's own standpoint, integration into a whole *vs.* differentiation into details, and hence seeks to implement professional realities. In such spirit, SGC's architecture provides a "game-based learning" framework along five interactive game levels:

1. learn content and pass quizzes
2. write and reflect about a personal standpoint
3. win with a team in a competitive discussion
4. negotiate a complex consensus between teams
5. integrate views when recognizing and analysing global long-term trends.

This set of game rules exhibits a framing condition for the expected process of social/societal self-organization. Students' motivation to earn better grades (*i.e.*, adding up the collected rewards) determines work attitude, team size, and individuals' tendency to adhere to strong personal convictions when constructing consensus. SGC's rules trigger two distinct processes: individual strife for good grades and social dynamics among peer students in class. These two goals create useful social dynamism during game play.

The emphasis within SGC is on rhythmic, gradually more complex social procedures in the group of participating learners who keep ever changing team compositions and research specialised fact-based arguments from the perspectives of all stakeholders informed. Participants (1) intellectually understand, (2) describe in writing and review each other, (3) engage in controversial debates, (4) try to find consensus solutions and finally (5) put into the wider context of global megatrends.

Since its invention in 2003, this web-based negotiation game has been implemented more than five dozen times and received positive feedback from students and co-teaching experts.

CONSENT FOR PUBLICATION

Not applicable.

CONFLICT OF INTEREST

The authors declare no conflict of interest, financial or otherwise.

ACKNOWLEDGEMENTS

Declared none.

REFERENCES

[1] G. Ahamer, and C. Schrei, "Exercise 'Technology Assessment' through a gaming procedure", *J. Design Res.,* vol. 5, no. 2, pp. 224-252, 2006.
[http://dx.doi.org/10.1504/JDR.2006.011364]

[2] M. McCracken, "Towards a typology of managerial barriers to learning", *J. Manage. Dev.,* vol. 24, no. 6, pp. 559-575, 2005.
[http://dx.doi.org/10.1108/02621710510601008]

[3] R. Tunstall, and M. Lynch, "The role of simulation case studies in enterprise education", *Educ. Train.,* vol. 52, no. 8/9, pp. 624-642, 2010.
[http://dx.doi.org/10.1108/00400911011088953]

[4] G. Ahamer, GIS^s and GIS^p facilitate higher education and cooperative learning design. *Handbook of Research on Transnational Higher Education Management.,* S. Mukerji, P. Tripathi, Eds., vol. I. IGI Global Publishers: USA, 2013, pp. 1-21.

[5] J.D. Owens, and L. Price, "Is e-learning replacing the traditional lecture?", *Educ. Train.,* vol. 52, no. 2, pp. 128-139, 2010.
[http://dx.doi.org/10.1108/00400911011027725]

[6] ÖGUT, "The Participation Manual", *Austrian Society for Environment and Technology (= Österreichische Gesellschaft für Umwelt und Technik),* Vienna, 2007. http://www.oegut.at/de/publikationen/liste.php?id=1406&ref_id=500

[7] M. Prensky, *Digital Game-Based Learning,* McGraw-Hill: New York, 2001. http://www.learningsim.com/content/lsnews/digital_game_learning.html

[8] U. Hytti, P. Stenholm, J. Heinonen, and J. Seikkula-Leino, "Perceived learning outcomes in entrepreneurship education: The impact of student motivation and team behaviour", *Educ. Train.,* vol. 52, no. 8/9, pp. 587-606, 2010.
[http://dx.doi.org/10.1108/00400911011088935]

[9] C.R. Rogers, *Freedom to Learn: A View of What Education Might Become.* Charles Merill: Columbus, Ohio, 1974.

[10] C. Rakos, E. Braun, and M. Nentwich, Technikbewertung und Umweltverträglichkeitsprüfung.*Band 1 der Schriftenreihe des Verbundkonzernes*Wien, 1988.

[11] G. Ossimitz, "Entwicklung systemischen Denkens – Theoretische Konzepte und empirische Untersuchungen", *Klagenfurter Beiträge zur Didaktik der Mathematik, Profil Verlag,* 2000.

[12] M. Kerres, *Multimediale und Telemediale Lernumgebungen – Konzeption und Entwicklung, Oldenburg Verlag,* 2000.

[13] A. Bork, "Adult education, lifelong learning, and the future", *Campus-Wide Inf. Syst.,* vol. 18, no. 5, pp. 195-203, 2001.
[http://dx.doi.org/10.1108/EUM0000000006266]

[14] M. Csikszentmihalyi, *Flow - psychology of optimal experience.* Harper and Row: New York, 1990.

[15] USW, "USW Reports – Umweltsystemwissenschaften (= Environmental Systems Science)", *Reports on implementations of Surfing Global Change,* 2010. http://www.uni-graz.at/usw1www/usw1www_magazin/usw1www_berichte.htm

[16] M. Montessori, *Kosmische Erziehung – Die Stellung des Menschen im Kosmos – Menschliche Potentialität und Erziehung,* Herder, 1996.

[17] S. Thiagarajan, *The 8-4-2-game,* Workshops by Thiagi, Inc, 2001.http://www.thiagi.com/

[18] W. Kolar, *"Technology Assessment: Grundlagen, methodische und organisatorische Probleme, Anwendungen",* Diplomarbeit an der Uni Linz, 1988.

[19] H. Barrows, "Is it Truly Possible to Have Such a Thing as dPBL (distributed Problem-Based Learning)?", *Distance Educ.,* vol. 23, no. 1, pp. 119-122, 2002.
[http://dx.doi.org/10.1080/01587910220124026]

[20] S. Naidu, A. Ip, and R. Linser, *Dynamic Goal-Based Role-Play Simulation on the Web-A Case Study,* University of Melbourne: Australia, 2003.http://www.roleplaysim.org/papers/Naidu_etal.html

[21] G. Ahamer, "Training to bridge multicultural geographies of perspectives", *Campus-Wide Inf. Syst.,* vol. 29, no. 1, pp. 21-44, 2011.
[http://dx.doi.org/10.1108/10650741211192037]

[22] HPS, *Stella 8.0, High Performance Systems,* 2003.http://www.hps-inc.com

[23] M. van Gelderen, "Autonomy as the guiding aim of entrepreneurship education", *Educ. Train.,* vol. 52, no. 8/9, pp. 710-721, 2010.
[http://dx.doi.org/10.1108/00400911011089006]

[24] A. Sivan, "The implementation of peer assessment: an action research approach", *Asess. Educ.,* vol. 7, no. 2, pp. 193-213, 2000.
[http://dx.doi.org/10.1080/713613328]

[25] F. Ronteltap, and A. Eurelings, "Activity and interaction of students in an electronic learning environment for Problem-Based Learning", *Dist. Educ.,* vol. 23, no. 1, pp. 11-22, 2002.
[http://dx.doi.org/10.1080/01587910220123955]

[26] V.M. Kern, L.M. Saraiva, and R. Pacheco, "Peer Review in Education: Promoting Collaboration, Written Expression, Critical Thinking, and Professional Responsibility", *Educ. Inf. Technol.,* vol. 8, no. 1, pp. 37-46, 2003.
[http://dx.doi.org/10.1023/A:1023974224315]

[27] D.A. Moreira, and E.Q. da Silva, "A Method to Increase Student Interaction Using Student Groups and Peer Review over the Internet", *Educ. Inf. Technol.,* vol. 8, no. 1, pp. 47-54, 2003.
[http://dx.doi.org/10.1023/A:1023926308385]

[28] D.A. Reilly, "The Power Politics Game: Offensive realism in theory and practice", *Simulation and Gaming: An Interdisciplinary Journal,* vol. 34, no. 2, pp. 298-305, 2003.
[http://dx.doi.org/10.1177/1046878103034002009]

[29] R.G. Schwartz, *Simulation and Gaming: An Interdisciplinary Journal,* vol. 33, no. 1, pp. 94-108, 2002.
[http://dx.doi.org/10.1177/1046878102033001006]

[30] G. Salter, "Comparing online and traditional teaching – a different approach", *Campus-Wide Inf. Syst.,* vol. 20, no. 3, pp. 137-145, 2003.
[http://dx.doi.org/10.1108/10650740310491306]

[31] K. Swan, "Building Learning Communities in Online Courses: the importance of interaction", *Educ. Commun. Inf.,* vol. 2, no. 1, pp. 23-49, 2002.
[http://dx.doi.org/10.1080/1463631022000005016]

[32] J.H.G. Klabbers, "Gaming and simulation: Principles of a science of design", *Simulation and Gaming: An Interdisciplinary Journal,* vol. 34, no. 4, pp. 569-591, 2003.
[http://dx.doi.org/10.1177/1046878103258205]

[33] J.J. Kirk, "The making of a gaming-simulation course: A personal tale", *Simulation and Gaming: An Interdisciplinary Journal,* vol. 35, no. 1, pp. 85-93, 2004.
[http://dx.doi.org/10.1177/1046878103261780]

[34] D. Myers, "Simulation, gaming, and the simulative", *Simulation and Gaming: An Interdisciplinary Journal,* vol. 30, no. 4, pp. 482-489, 1999.
[http://dx.doi.org/10.1177/104687819903000406]

[35] D.L. Meadows, "Tools for understanding the limits to growth: Comparing a simulation and a game", *Simulation and Gaming: An Interdisciplinary Journal,* vol. 32, no. 4, pp. 522-536, 2001.
[http://dx.doi.org/10.1177/104687810103200408]

[36] J. Blewitt, "Higher education for a sustainable world", *Educ. Train.,* vol. 52, no. 8/9, pp. 477-488, 2010.
[http://dx.doi.org/10.1108/00400911011068432]

CHAPTER 5

Research-Based Proposals on Optical Spectroscopy in Secondary School

Daniele Buongiorno[1,*] and Marisa Michelini[1]

[1] *URDF (Unità di Ricerca in Didattica della Fisica) - Università degli Studi di Udine Via delle Scienze 206, 33100 Udine, Italy*

Abstract: The interpretation of spectra, particularly in the optical band, is a conceptual and historical link between classical and modern physics. It is an empiric proof of the atomic structure of matter and an experimental instrument to investigate phenomena involving interactions between light and matter. On a disciplinary plan regarding physics, it is a fundamental contribution; unfortunately, the road to embed optical spectroscopy in a coherent educational pattern is still long.

From a research perspective, the Physics Education Research Unit from Udine University focused on the design of an educational path on spectroscopy for high school students, with the aim of involving them in interpretative challenges, both theoretical and experimental, in order to recognize the connection between the microscopic energetic structure for matter and the emission of radiation, with particular emphasis in the optical band.

The Model of Educational Reconstruction framed the design of the educational path. Based on limited but significant literature on the interpretation of optical spectra by university and secondary school students, we designed different intervention modules in which interpretative issues are problematized using Inquiry-Based Learning strategies. Using Design-Based Research methodologies, seven different experimentations were carried out, monitoring learning outcomes of 208 students aged 17-18 by empirical research methods.

Keywords: Design-based research, Educational reconstruction, Optical spectroscopy, Physics education research.

INTRODUCTION

Modern physics is considered a key content in majority of EU secondary school curricula, but, nowadays issues concerning modalities, contents, instruments and

---

[*] Corresponding author Daniele Buongiorno: URDF (Unità di Ricerca in Didattica della Fisica) - Università degli Studi di Udine, Via delle Scienze 206, 33100 Udine, Italy; Tel: +39 3398424547;
E-mail: buongiornodaniele@gmail.com

Maria Teresa Caccamo and Salvatore Magazù (Eds.)
All rights reserved-© 2021 Bentham Science Publishers

methods to integrate these topics in the well-established teaching praxis are open problems. The current approach is quite often limited to the storytelling of the main crucial aspects and experimental contradictions with classical physics that characterized the beginning of the XX century, rather than an approach founding a scientific culture taking into account the instruments and methods of physics [1].

In the wider framework of modern physics, optical spectroscopy provides the experimental basis of the modern quantum theory and it represents an emblematic context in which physics interprets information to build a model.

A complete and coherent educational path on optical spectroscopy for high school students will be presented here: various experimental activities support the interpretations of microscopic phenomena related to light-matter interaction and actively engage the students, in order to help them develop a functional understanding of the connection between energy levels in atoms and the emitted light.

The proposal aims at overcoming the learning difficulties and preconceptions that literature evidenced.

THE RESEARCH PERSPECTIVE

The starting point for design a research-based educational proposal is the analysis of literature concerning the most common conceptual knots or learning difficulties expressed directly or indirectly, by students on the chosen topic. Difficulties in understanding spectra emerged in both secondary school and university students, and they are related to the connection between spectral lines and atomic levels, and the experimental setting that can produce a spectrum. In particular, students often associate the energy of a specific emission line in a spectrum with the energy of a specific energy level, rather than to the difference between couple of levels [2, 3]. This problem has slightly different aspects: the fundamental level is not considered a level or involved in every transition [4 - 7]. Despite spectroscopic measurements have a pivotal role in astronomy, introductory astronomy students show various kinds of preconceptions and conceptual incoherencies regarding the way in which atoms and radiation interact [8]. Research shows that, in the case of high school students, this is due to a not coherent quantum model for both matter and radiation [10]. University students believe that the energy of radiation is linked to intensity rather than to the colour [9]. Erroneous models have to be tested to highlight strengths and weaknesses in order to build a usable and coherent model describing the phenomenology [11, 12].

According to the theoretical framework of the Model of Educational Reconstruction (MER) [13, 14] the approach for teaching any topic implies that the contents have to be "reconstructed" from an educational point of view. This takes into account several aspects: the main conceptual difficulties have to be analyzed, as well as the main interpretative obstacles as emerged from the historical development of physics. This supports the design of educational sub-phases representing different stages of the educational path, in which active learning strategies produce the overcoming of the conceptual knots and the appropriation of the founding disciplinary elements by means of Design-Based Research (DBR) methods [15 - 18].

THE GENERAL STRUCTURE OF THE EDUCATIONAL PATH

In order to activate an effective learning process, a good starting point is the exploration of students' spontaneous ideas concerning simple observations [19]. The path thus starts considering the sorting of optical phenomena in three huge thematic areas concerning light: production, propagation and matter-interaction. Transmission and refraction show how different points of view are taken into account in describing apparently similar phenomena: in refraction, only the macroscopic change in direction is taken into account, while in transmission the microscopic interactions between light and matter are involved. Presenting different light sources reinforces the interpretation according to which the generation of light implies an energetic transformation (Fig. **1**) inside the source.

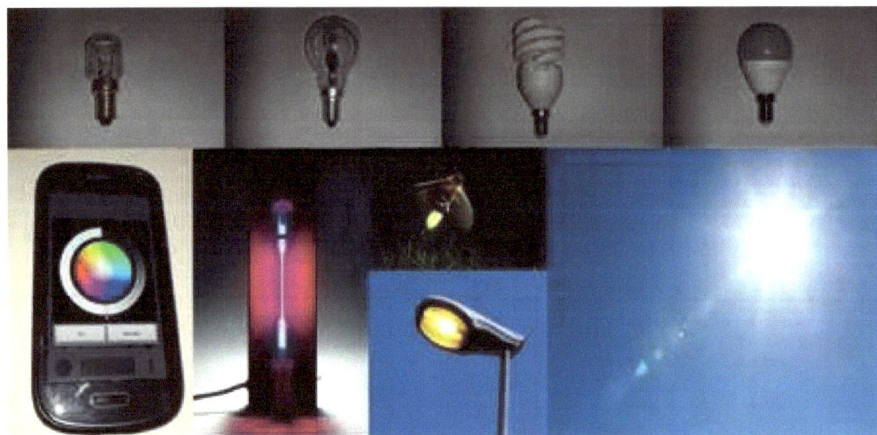

Fig. (1). Various types of light sources are shown in the path: a light source is seen as a system able to convert a specific form of energy into radiant energy; thus an energetic transformation is involved every time light is generated.

Students classify different sources according to their spectra: continuous, discrete and banded, using simple cardboard spectroscopes. The role of each part of the spectroscope is analyzed with the artefact method [20] in order to identify the operative role of every component (Fig. 2). The functioning of the diffraction grating, which operates a sort of decomposition of light, will be formalized in the following path.

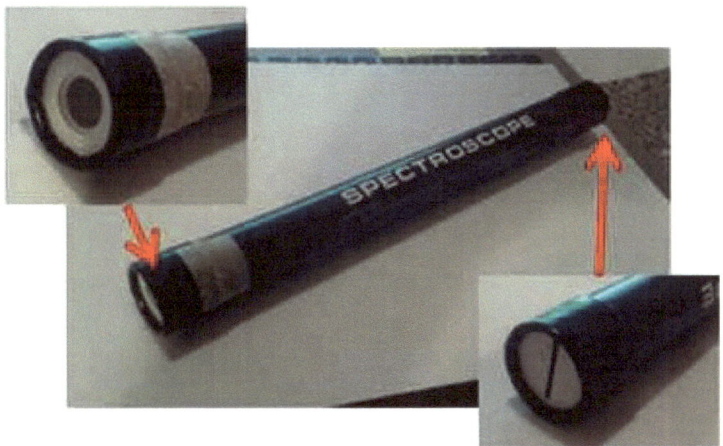

Fig. (2). A simple spectroscope: light enters into the instruments through the slit, and the grating decomposes its colours.

The experimental study of single and multiple slit diffraction is performed with digital acquisition of light intensity as a function of the position [21] which gives diffraction the role of dispersive mechanism able to highlight the chromatic structure of light (Fig. 3, right). The colours turn out to be measurable quantities using wavelengths or energies. In some experimentations, the analysis of the diffraction pattern took place with IBL strategy [22] in which students themselves design an experiment, obtaining the laws and relations describing the observed diffraction patterns (Fig. 3, left) individuating variables and parameters.

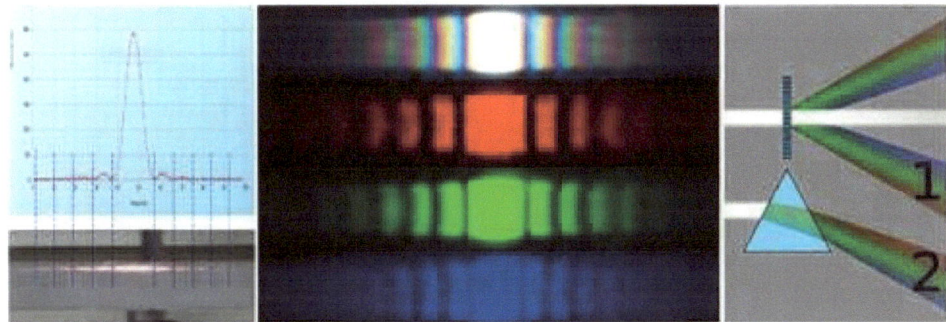

Fig. (3). Diffraction and dispersion can be used to reveal the chromatic structure of light. The colour emerges to be a parameter upon which such phenomena depend on.

The path takes into account flame tests, an evidence of the link between the different structure of the source and the light that is emitted. The problem of the interpretation of the phenomenon is posed: why are only certain colours/energies visible? How does the structure of an atom affect the emitted light pattern? (Fig. 4).

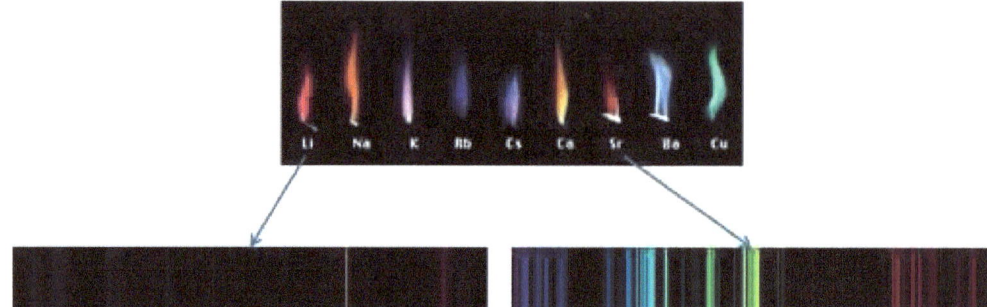

Fig. (4). Flame tests.

Once a spectrum is defined, as the series of colours that appears in a certain order of the diffraction pattern, an analysis of the Balmer series for hydrogen is proposed as a context to search for regularities in the observed spectrum (Fig. 5). The historical reasoning is reconstructed by students that realize that the coefficients obtained by Balmer can be represented by the general empirical formula $ën=k·n2n2-4$, that is subsequently re-elaborated for obtaining a more general and interpretable one, in terms of wave-numbers: $1ën=k'·14-1n2$, as Rydberg did [23].

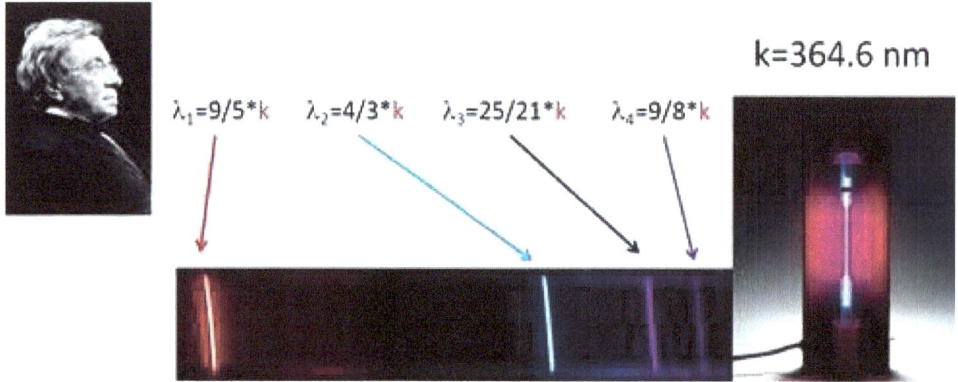

Fig. (5). In the hydrogen spectrum, different wavelengths are multiple quantities of a constant. Balmer's coefficients, ratios of integers, opens the interpretation of the energetic structure of the atom.

Rydberg's formula and the interpretation of the photoelectric effect, relating energy and wavenumbers, suggest students interpreting how a luminous emission in a spectrum is caused by an energetic variation in the emitting system, *i.e.* in the atom. The idea that spectra characterizes the atoms emerges naturally at this stage, since every atom has a different structure, thus a different spectrum. The model making use of physical discrete orbits (the Bohr model) is neglected to emphasize the idea that a specific energy level does not correspond to an orbit, rather to a specific state of the atom. This allows discussing with students that an atom is a system, able to emit light, with a specific set of energetic possibilities. No needs for classical orbits emerges, and this help in the future perspective of building a more realistic quantum model for every atom.

CONTEXT, SAMPLE AND METHODOLOGY

The proposal was experimented with 208 17-18 years-old students from Italian scientific high schools. All activities were within IDIFO6 project[2] of the national project PLS (Progetto Lauree Scientifiche - Scientific Degree Project). The experimentations have been set in three different contexts:

- **Masterclass**: 8-hours activity to the University, alternatively discussion of the path and experimental activities.
- **CLOE** (Conceptual Laboratory of Operative Exploration): this activity has the same setting of a masterclass, but students are involved only for 4 hours.
- **Summer school on modern physics**: talented students attend a 6-days activity at University comprising frontal lessons, experimental activities and educational path on different aspects of modern physics. The spectroscopy module occupies a total of 8 hours.

Laboratorial activities were embedded in the educational path ad were carried out in groups: the optical goniometer experiment, the LED-ruler experiment (described hereafter) and on-line diffraction measures from a single slit.

- **The optical goniometer experiment**. A discrete spectra from a gas-discharge lamp is observed. The goniometer (Fig. **6**) allows the measure of the angles corresponding to the various emissions, making possible to evaluate the wavelength, or the corresponding energy, of a specific emission.
- **The LED-ruler experiment.** Low-cost materials allow observing the spectrum of a coloured LED: the light source is sighted through diffraction toy glasses, and the virtual image of its spectrum is projected along a ruler. A simple calculation is used to the energy corresponding to the dominant colour: its diffraction angle is geometrically evaluated, and the corresponding colour energy can be calculated (Fig. **7**). This value is related with the triggering voltage of the LED, highlighting the energy nature of the colours.

- **Diffraction measurements with a digital sensor**. Single slit diffraction is analysed with a patented sensor [21], which allows obtaining a digital plot of light intensity *versus* position along the screen. Analysing the obtained diffraction pattern allows to experimentally obtain the laws governing the phenomenon.

The different interventions followed slightly different trajectories: contents and their sequence in every experimentations are modified and fine-tuned time by time, as imposed by a DBR methodologies (Table **1**).

Table 1. Lineouts of the different interventions, referring to last column in Table 2. Every column refers to a different intervention (M: masterclass, C: CLOE, SS: summer school); numbers refers to the order of the contents embedded in every path, which shared the same conceptual core.

CONTENTS	M(a)	M(b)	M(c)	C(a)	C(b)	M(d)	SS
Light sources	1	1	1	1	2	2	1
Light emitted from sources	2	2	2	2	1	1	2
Diffraction	-	-	-	4	5	5	5
IBL path on diffraction	4	4	4	-	-	-	-
Exploration with spectroscopes	5	5	5	5	3	4	3
Structure of a spectroscope	6	6	6	6	4	5	4
Coloured light structure	3	3	3	3	-	3	7
Planck's hypothesis and Bohr's model	7	9	9	9	8	9	9
Total energy of an H atom	8	7	7	7	6	7	6
From coefficient to Balmer's formula	-	-	-	-	-	-	8
Balmer-Rydberg's formula ($1/\lambda$)	-	8	8	-	-	-	-
Balmer-Rydberg's formula (energy)	-	-	-	8	7	8	10
Black body emission formalism	-	-	-	-	-	-	9
Drawings of levels and prevision of emissions	-	10	10	10	9	10	11
From discrete spectra to levels	-	-	-	-	-	11	12

Different monitoring instruments have been used in different experimentations (Table **2**). Every student completed a tutorial, guiding the reasoning, following the structure of the path and a post-test, and in few cases a pre-test. In particular, the post-test was structured in 13 questions (Table **3**) grouped in conceptual categories. Pre- and post-test were identical only in the summer school experimentation.

Table 2. In every experimentation different educational path were proposed. Context, student sample and monitoring instruments varied from time to time. As imposed by DBR methodologies, the path underwent variations in both contents and structure, as highlighted in the last column.

Date	Experimentation	N. Students	Pre-Test	Tutorial	Post-Test	Path Version
Jan, 1, 2017	M(a)	43	No	Yes	Yes	1
Feb, 1, 2017	M(b)	33	Yes	Yes	Yes	2
Feb, 2, 2017	M(c)	35	Yes	Yes	Yes	2
Feb, 13, 2017	C(a)	22	No	Yes	Yes	3
Feb, 14, 2017	C(b)	32	No	Yes	Yes	4
Mar, 10, 2017	M(d)	11	No	Yes	Yes	5
Jun, 28, 2017	SS	32	Yes	No	Yes	6

Table 3. Requests in the post-test.

Questions	Requests
D1	Point out similarities and differences among various observed spectra and justification
D2	Explain the emission process causing the observed emission lines
D3-D5	Describe the role of the grating and the slit
D6-D7	Describe the light emission process from an atom comparing the energies of the emitted radiation and those of the levels
D8	Represent a spectrum knowing the energetic structure of the levels
D9-D12	Obtain the level structure given a discrete spectrum
D13	Represent energetic structure of a LED and a gas discharge lamp given their emission spectra

DATA ANALYSIS

Here we report the complete and detailed research results of the various experimentations. .A preliminary study has been described in [24,25]. Qualitative methods have been used in order to analyze students' written answers in the sense that both written answers and drawings have been classified in categories, refined upon the aspects noted a-posteriori. Each category was defined operationally using students' own words and expressions. The categories that emerged in this way allowed data interpretation, consisting in an analysis of the frequencies in each category. As suggested by qualitative analysis methods, in order to give meaning ambiguous or apparently no-sensed answers, using clues present in answers to different questions was necessary.

Hereafter the answers at the most significant questions of the post-test from the experimentation "Masterclass(c)" and at the most significant question in pre- and post-test from the experimentation conducted in the summer school will be discussed.

Masterclass(c) Experimentation: Post-test

D1: "Point out similarities and differences between light spectra from an incandescent lamp, a gas-discharge lamp and a LED, justifying the main differences."

D2: "In the experiment of the optical goniometer, explain the process accounting for the observation of spectral lines, with the aid of a sketch."

D3-D5: "It is investigated the functional role of the slit and of the grating in accounting for the formation of a spectrum."

D8: "The values of the first five energy level of ionized helium atom are shown and students are asked to represent them graphically and to sketch out the spectrum they expect to observe."

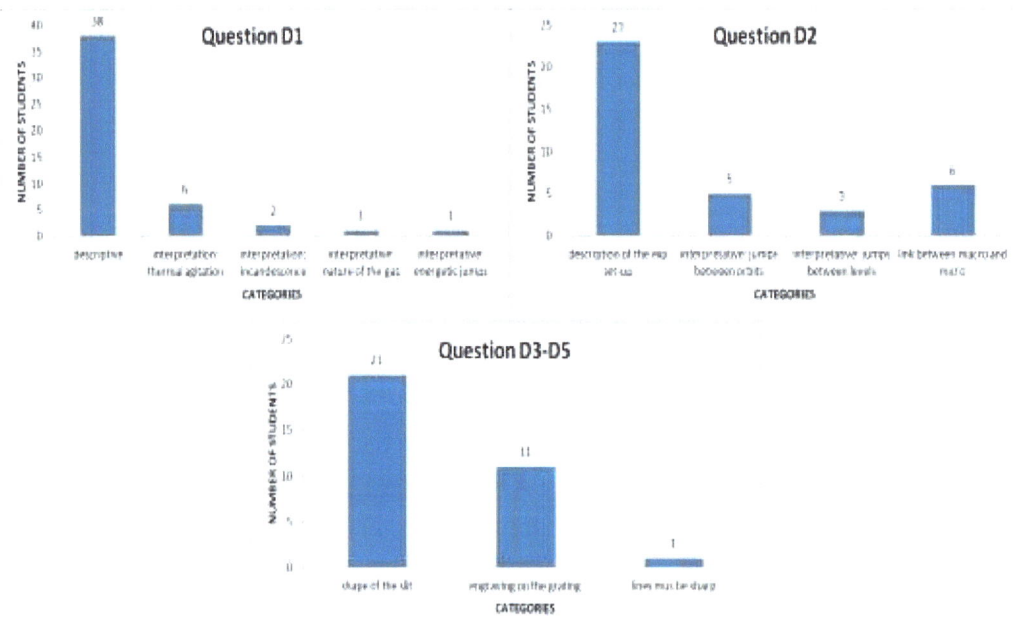

Fig. (8). Analysis of answers to questions D1, D2 and D3-D5.

Concerning question D1 (Fig. **8**, top left) answers are mainly limited to describe spectra in terms of colours and/or present discontinuities, making analogies with the rainbow colours. Thermal agitation or incandescence is quoted by a minority of the sample in order to account for continuous spectrum. The interpretation of a line spectrum due of the nature of the emitting gas or energetic jumps at atomic levels is present in few answers without any specifications of the used mental model.

Answers to question D2 (Fig. **8**, top right) contains mainly the description of the experiment in functional terms, eventually quoting diffraction as the mechanism responsible for the division of the colours. About 20% of students interpret the evidence of different lines adopting the model that use transitions between levels and orbits. A link between a microscopic interpretation with the measurements apparatus is made by a minority of the sample. It emerges how the Bohr orbit model, which is used to describe jumps between orbits and/or indirectly used to account for the idea that an electron is localizable, is a conceptual referent for many students.

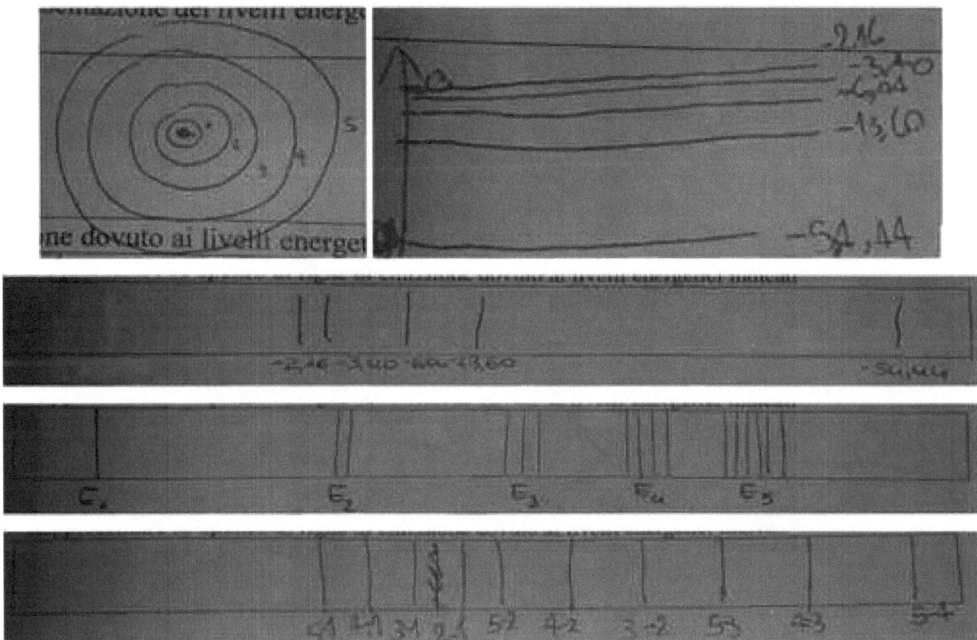

Fig. (9). Models for atomic energy levels: orbits (top left) and levels stacked with respect to an energy scale (top right). Given 5 levels, students expect 5 emissions in the spectrum, n close lines associated with n^{th} level or all possible transitions.

In question D3-D5 (Fig. **8**, bottom) about half of the sample associate the shape of the slit with the shape of the lines, while about 20% of the students believe that the engraving on the grating are responsible for it. A single student employs the sharpness of the lines as a fundamental conceptual referent in a description of a discrete spectrum, independently from the shape of the slit.

Concerning question D8, 38% of students employs a model representing stacked levels as a general representation for the energetic structure of an atom avoiding the using its spatial representation, while 17% students employs orbits as conceptual referents (Fig. **9**, top). Three main models emerge relating spectral lines and the structure of the atom (Fig. **9**, bottom): a) 1:1 correspondence between a line and a level (53%), b) n close lines associated with n^{th} level (9%) and (c) all possible transitions (2%).

Summer School Experimentation: Pre- and Post-Test

D1: "What do single energy levels represent in an atomic model?" and D2: "Considering the first six energy levels of the hydrogen atom (whose values are provided) how many emissions are expected? Justify the answer and draw the spectrum." Answers to D1 in the pre-test are mainly given in terms of spatial localization of electrons in atoms, rather than in terms of proprieties of electrons, probably due to scholastic background.

NR	N	SPATIAL LOCALIZATION			
		Orbits	Orbitals	Distance from nucleus	Space occupied by electrons
7	32 (PRE)	13	2	1	4
1	31 (POST)	2	2	3	4

	N	PROPERTIES OF ELECTRONS			
		Energies	Energies in the orbital	Excitation	It doesn't emit
	32 (PRE)	3	1	3	0
	31 (POST)	5	1	9	4

	N	CHARACTERISTIC ENERGY		
		Photon energy	Difference between levels=energy emitted	Characteristic energy values of the system
	32 (PRE)	1	1	0
	31 (POST)	1	5	6

Fig. (**10**). Comparison between pre and post-test to question D1.

A minority of students defines energy levels as the energy of the emitted photons or noting that a difference between the energy of two levels corresponds to the emitted energy. The post-test shows a general trend against a description in spatial terms of the electrons: the path promotes the perspective of a general model for atoms in terms of characteristics energies of the emitting system, rather than a more restrictive and limitative spatial description using orbits (Fig. **10**).

The idea according to which a single level corresponds to a single emission line was quite popular before the intervention, as shown by analysis of answers to D2 (Fig. **11**). The model predicting that a spectral line is the outcome of a transition between a couple of level is shared by 38% students; in particular, 8 of them consider all the transitions, 3 students consider only the ones involving the fundamental level and 1 student considers only transitions involving adjacent levels. After the intervention, arbitrary models are overcome, since it emerges from the post-test that all students adopt the model according to which all transitions have to be taken into account, since there is no reason to exclude some of them.

N	1 line = 1 level	1 line = 1 transition		
		All	Only to F.L.	Between adjacent levels
32 (PRE)	13*	8	3	1
31 (POST)	-	31	-	-

* One student does not take into account for the fundamental level.

Fig. (**11**). Comparison between pre and post-test to question D2.

CONCLUSIONS

Having chosen optical spectroscopy as the research topic, an educational path for secondary school students has been designed and experimented in different contexts. Learning outcomes have been here presented and discussed, in particular focusing on the following aspects: which microscopic models spontaneously emerge in order to describe discrete emissions from matter in the context of experimental explorations; the spontaneous ideas about spectral lines and energy levels; the operative obstacles linked to the experimental set-up.

The theoretical framework of the MER and DBR methods guided the design and implementation and testing of the educational path from a research perspective. From student's answers analysis, the path, enriched with the experimental activities, is able to stimulate them in changing from a simplified descriptive plan to an aware interpretative plan.

The different versions of the path may represent the basis for overcoming the main conceptual knots evidenced in the literature; in particular, regarding models, scholastic praxis usually takes into account different models for atoms (Thomson, Rutherford, Bohr, Schrodinger) and different conceptual referents (orbit, orbital, energy states, *etc*...). The above-mentioned experimentations emphasize the need of underline and clarify strengths and weaknesses of every model. Moreover, it emerged the need of considering not only the specific case of the hydrogen atom, in which the correspondence between orbits and levels is direct (but misleading!) but also more general cases, in which atoms are described as a set of allowed energetic values, allowing a more general and physical description of how matter and radiation interact.

CONSENT FOR PUBLICATION

Not applicable.

CONFLICT OF INTEREST

The authors declare no conflict of interest, financial or otherwise.

ACKNOWLEDGEMENTS

Declared none.

REFERENCES

[1] M. Michelini, "Teaching modern physics in secondary school", *Proc. Science (FFP14)*, 2014. art. n. 231.

[2] N.S. Rebello, C. Cumaranatunge, L.T. Escalada, D.A. Zollman, and D. Donnelly, "Simulating the spectra of light source", *Comput. Phys.*, vol. 12, no. 1, pp. 28-33, 1998.
[http://dx.doi.org/10.1063/1.168684]

[3] D.A. Zollman, and N.S. Rebello, *Am. J. Phys.*, vol. 70, no. 3, pp. 252-259, 2002.
[http://dx.doi.org/10.1119/1.1435347]

[4] N.D. Korhasan, and L. Wang, "Students' mental models of atomic spectra", *Chem. Educ. Res. Pract*, vol. 17, 2016.

[5] L. Ivanjek, *"An investigation of conceptual understanding of atomic spectra among university students"*, Ph.D. thesis, The University of Zagreb, 2012.

[6] L. Ivanjek, S.P. Shaffer, L.C. McDermott, M. Planinic, and D. Veza, "Research as a guide for curriculum development: An example from introductory spectroscopy. I. Identifying student difficulties with atomic emission spectra", *Am. J. Phys.*, vol. 83, no. 1, pp. 85-90, 2015.
[http://dx.doi.org/10.1119/1.4901977]

[7] L. Ivanjek, S.P. Shaffer, L.C. McDermott, M. Planinic, and D. Veza, "Research as a guide for curriculum development: An example from introductory spectroscopy. II. Addressing student difficulties with atomic emission spectra", *Am. J. Phys.*, vol. 83, no. 2, pp. 171-178, 2015.
[http://dx.doi.org/10.1119/1.4902222]

[8] E.M. Bardar, E.E. Prather, K. Brecher, and T.S. Slater, "The need for a light and spectroscopy concept

inventory for assessing innovations in introductory astronomy survey courses", *Astron. Educ. Rev.,* vol. 4, no. 2, pp. 20-27, 2006.
[http://dx.doi.org/10.3847/AER2005018]

[9] S. Lee, *"Students' understanding of spectra"*, Ph.D. thesis, The University of Kansas State, 2002.

[10] F. Savall-Alemany, J.L. Domènech-Blanco, and J. Guisasola, "Identifying student and teacher difficulties in interpreting atomic spectra using a quantum model of emission and absorption of radiation", *Phys. Rev. ST Phys. Ed. Res,* vol. 12, no. 1, 2016. art. n. 01013.

[11] J.K. Gilbert, C. Boulter, and M. Rutherford, "Models in explanations, part 1: Horses for courses?", *Int. J. Sci. Educ.,* vol. 20, no. 1, pp. 83-97, 1998.
[http://dx.doi.org/10.1080/0950069980200106]

[12] J.K. Gilbert, C. Boulter, and M. Rutherford, "Models in explanations, part 2: Whose voice, whose ears?", *Int. J. Sci. Educ.,* vol. 20, no. 2, pp. 187-203, 1998.
[http://dx.doi.org/10.1080/0950069980200205]

[13] R. Duit, H. Gropengießer, and U. Kattmann, Towards science education research that is relevant for improving practice: The Model of Educational Reconstruction.*Developing Standards in Research on Science Education* ed. H.E. Fischer, London, Taylor & Francis, 2005.

[14] R. Duit, H. Gropengießer, U. Kattmann, and M. Komorek, "The Model of Educational Reconstruction - a framework for improving teaching and learning science", *Science Education Research and Practice in Europe,* ed. D. Jorde J. Dillon, Rotterdam, Sense Publishers, 2012.

[15] D.B.R. Collective, "Design-based research: An emerging paradigm for educational inquiry", *Educ. Res.,* vol. 32, no. 1, pp. 5-8, 2003.
[http://dx.doi.org/10.3102/0013189X032001005]

[16] A. Collins, D. Joseph, and K. Bielaczyc, "Design research: Theoretical and methodological issues", *J. Learn. Sci.,* vol. 13, no. 1, pp. 15-42, 2004.
[http://dx.doi.org/10.1207/s15327809jls1301_2]

[17] J. Van der Akker, K. Gravemeijer, and S. McKennedy S., *Educational Design Research. Routledge.,* N. Nieveen, Ed., London, New York, 2006.
[http://dx.doi.org/10.4324/9780203088364]

[18] T. Anderson, and J. Shattuck, "Design-Based Research: A Decade of Progress in Education Research?", *Educ. Res.,* vol. 41, no. 1, pp. 16-25, 2012.
[http://dx.doi.org/10.3102/0013189X11428813]

[19] L. Viennot, Relating research in didactics and actual teaching practice: impact and virtues of critical details.*Science Education Research in the Knowledge-Based Society.,* D. Psillos, Ed., 2003.
[http://dx.doi.org/10.1007/978-94-017-0165-5_40]

[20] M.G. Bartolini Bussi, and M.A. Mariotti, "Semiotic mediation: from history to mathematics classroom", *For Learn. Math.,* vol. 19, no. 2, pp. 27-35, 1999.

[21] M. Gervasio, M. Michelini, and A. Lucegrafo, "USB Data Acquisition System", *MPTL14 Proc,* Lamboune B. *et al.* (Ed.), 2009. http://www.fisica.uniud.it/URDF/ mptl14/contents.htm

[22] M. Michelini, and A. Stefanel, "Upper secondary students face optical diffraction using simple experiments and on-line measurements", *FFP14 Proc,* 2015

[23] W.R. Hindmarsh, and D. Ter Haar, *Atomic Spectra.* Pergamon Press, 1967.

[24] D. Buongiorno, and M. Michelini, "An educational path on optical spectroscopy as a bridge from classical to modern Physics to overcome conceptual knots", *Conference Proceedings,* 2018 9789995714369

[25] D. Buongiorno, and M. Michelini, Research-Based Path Proposal on Optical Spectroscopy in Secondary School. *Fundamental Physics and Physics Education Research.*, B.G. Sidharth, J.C. Murillo, M. Michelini, C. Perea, Eds., Springer: Cham, 2021.
[http://dx.doi.org/10.1007/978-3-030-52923-9_19]

CHAPTER 6

Normal Mode Investigation of a System of Coupled Oscillators: a Physics Lecture

Maria Teresa Caccamo[1,*] and **Salvatore Magazù**[1]

[1] *Dipartimento di Scienze Matematiche e Informatiche, Scienze Fisiche e Scienze della Terra, Università di Messina, Viale Ferdinando Stagno D'Alcontres n°31, S. Agata, 98166, Messina, Italy*

Abstract: In this work the contents of an academic lecture addressed to first year Physics students on a system of coupled oscillators is presented. More specifically, the physical system dealt is constituted by two oscillating masses interacting through a connecting spring. At first, the theory describing the system dynamics is presented by putting into evidence how the diagonalization process allows to reduce the coupled oscillation equations to formally simpler, but physically equivalent, expressions which make reference to uncoupled oscillations and how the new chosen coordinates do not refer to the positions of the real masses but describe collective properties of the system, namely its normal modes. To facilitate the comprehension of the analytical procedure, an experiment addressed to characterize the system normal mode frequencies is proposed. On this purpose, for analysing the oscillation amplitude as a function of time, a comparison between Fourier Transform and Wavelet Transform is presented. What it emerges is that, differently from what occurs for Fourier Transform which provides a value of the motion average frequency, the Wavelet Transform allows to simultaneously execute a time–frequency analysis.

Keywords: Coupled oscillators, Fourier Transform, Wavelet Transform.

INTRODUCTION

As a rule, to improve the understanding of a Physics topic, it is important to integrate theory with experiments [1 - 3]. Indeed, the process of planning and executing an experiment, which also includes the elaboration and interpretation of data, the formulation of empirical laws (*i.e.* primary model), and the comparison with a theory's outputs, is extremely formative, because it forces the student to be no longer a spectator, more or less passive, but the protagonist of a creative and significant work [4 - 9]. Therefore, the empirical dimension of Physics is a fundamental element of the teaching endeavour and experiments assume relevant

---

[*] **Corresponding author Maria Teresa Caccamo:** Dipartimento di Scienze Matematiche e Informatiche, Scienze Fisiche e Scienze della Terra, Università di Messina, Viale Ferdinando Stagno D'Alcontres n°31, S. Agata, 98166, Messina, Italy; Tel: +39 0906765019; E-mail: mcaccamo@unime.it

Maria Teresa Caccamo and Salvatore Magazù (Eds.)
All rights reserved-© 2021 Bentham Science Publishers

importance [10 - 15]. For this purpose, one can assert that a scientific theory can only have the scope it has if it is in contact with the real world that proves its validity and significance. Moreover, the scientific construction consists of an incessant, mutual and oscillating connection between the theoretical moment and the experimental moment. A scientific experiment is a procedure that makes a certain effect investigable and analysable in circumstances prepared according to a severed plan and according to certain hypotheses relating to the possible effects [16 - 21].

Therefore, the main purpose of a Physics experiment is specifically to trace a significant didactic itinerary that allows reaching the law of a physical phenomenon starting from a series of measures of physical quantities, detected experimentally during a physical laboratory activity. In other words, the aim is to experimentally research the physical-mathematical correlation existing between some characteristic variables of the phenomenon under examination through inductive procedures that highlight, in a clear and significant way, the empirical nature of Physics [22 - 25]. The experiment is nothing more than a physical study of a phenomenon, obtained by analysing the phenomenon itself in terms of quantitative investigation (Fig. **1**).

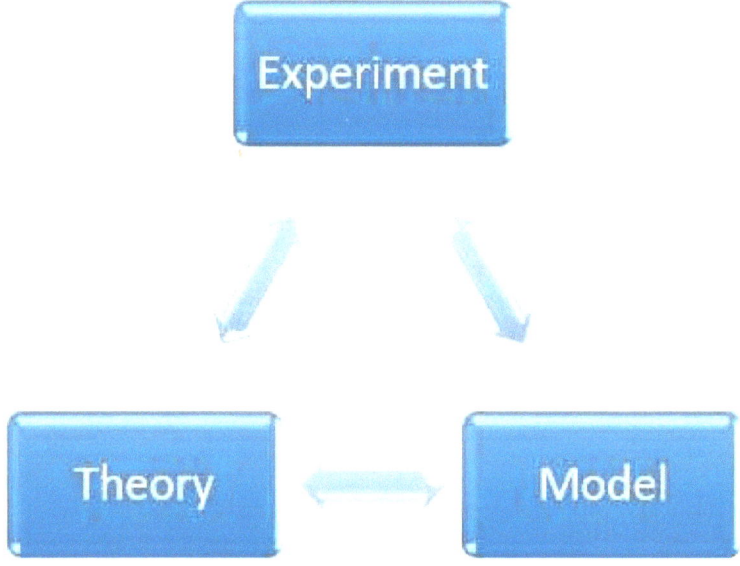

Fig. (1). A sketch of the joint employment of Theory, Experiment and Model.

Within this framework, with the aim of planning a Physics lecture addressed to first year academic students, in the present work, an integrated approach based on joint employment of theory and experiment sections is proposed. The subject of the lecture concerns a physical system constituted by two oscillating masses interacting through a connecting spring.

The developed theory and the experiment are both addressed to characterize the in-phase and out of phase normal modes of system. For this purpose, a comparison of Fourier Transform (FT) and Wavelet Transform (WT) is also presented. It will be highlighted how, FT furnishes only the motion average frequency value, while WT performs a time–frequency analysis [26 - 31]. The advantages and disadvantages of the two analysis approaches are also discussed.

THEORETICAL BACKGROUND

Let's consider two oscillating masses that interact through a connecting spring. The mass values, *m*, and the spring constants, *k*, are identical (Fig. 2).

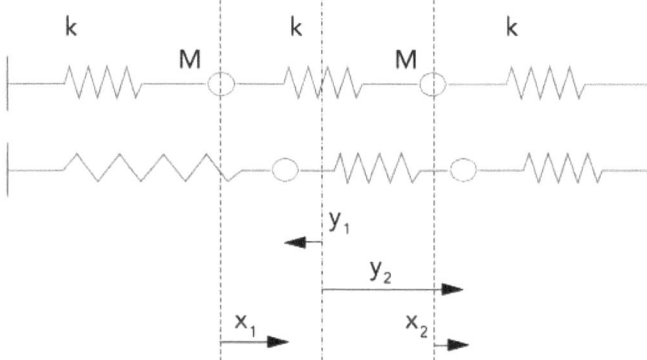

Fig. (2). System of two coupled oscillators.

Let's indicate with x_1 the displacement of the first mass from its equilibrium position, *i.e.* x_1 corresponds to the elongation or the contraction of the first spring (starting from the left); let's indicate with x_2 the displacement of the second mass from its equilibrium position, *i.e.* x_2 is the elongation or the contraction of the third spring [32, 33].

By employing Newton's second law, one can write, starting from Hooke's law [34 - 36]:

$$\begin{cases} m\ddot{x}_1 = -kx_1 + k(x_2 - x_1) \\ m\ddot{x}_2 = -kx_2 - k(x_2 - x_1) \end{cases} \quad (1)$$

and then:

$$\begin{cases} m\ddot{x}_1 = -kx_1 + kx_2 - kx_1 \\ m\ddot{x}_2 = -kx_2 - kx_2 - kx_1 \end{cases} \quad (2)$$

$$\begin{cases} m\ddot{x}_1 = -2kx_1 + kx_2 \\ m\ddot{x}_2 = -2kx_2 + kx_1 \end{cases} \quad (3)$$

To solve this system, we perform both the sum and the difference of the two equations.

By adding the two equations of eq. (3), one obtains:

$$m\ddot{x}_1 + m\ddot{x}_2 = -2kx_1 + kx_2 - 2kx_2 + kx_1 \quad (4)$$

$$m(\ddot{x}_1 + \ddot{x}_2) = -k(x_1 + x_2) \quad (5)$$

By executing the variable change $\xi = x_1 + x_2$, eqn. 5 can be reformulated as $m\ddot{\xi} = -k\xi$, whose solution is:

$$x_1 + x_2 = A_1 \cos(\omega_1 t + \varphi_1), \quad \omega_1 = \sqrt{\frac{k}{m}} \quad (6)$$

which furnishes:

$$x_1 + x_2 = A_1 \cos(\omega_1 t + \varphi_1), \quad \omega_1 = \sqrt{\frac{k}{m}} \quad (7)$$

On the other hand, by taking the difference between the two equations (3), one has:

$$m(\ddot{x}_2 - \ddot{x}_1) = -2kx_2 + kx_1 + 2kx_1 - kx_2 \quad (8)$$

$$m(\ddot{x}_2 - \ddot{x}_1) = -3kx_2 + 3kx_1 \tag{9}$$

$$m(\ddot{x}_2 - \ddot{x}_1) = -3k(x_2 - x_1) \tag{10}$$

Also, in this case, by performing a variable change with $\xi = x_2 - x_1$, eqn. 10 becomes $m\ddot{\xi} = -k\xi$, that is again the equation of a harmonic oscillator, whose solution is:

$$x_2 - x_1 = A_2\cos(\omega_2 t + \varphi_2), \quad \omega_2 = \sqrt{\frac{3k}{m}} \tag{11}$$

Therefore, we have two solutions that oscillate with two fixed frequency ω_1 and ω_2. More precisely since $\omega_2 > \omega_1$, ω_1 can be defined as the slow mode and ω_2 the fast mode. These solutions are not other than the normal modes for the investigated systems [37 - 39]. The general solution can be then written as a linear combination of the two solutions:

$$\begin{aligned} x_1 &= \frac{1}{2}[(x_1 + x_2) + (x_2 - x_1)] \\ &= \frac{1}{2}[A_1\cos(\omega_1 t + \varphi_1) + A_2\cos(\omega_2 t + \varphi_2)] \end{aligned} \tag{12}$$

$$\begin{aligned} x_2 &= \frac{1}{2}[(x_1 + x_2) - (x_2 - x_1)] \\ &= \frac{1}{2}[A_1\cos(\omega_1 t + \varphi_1) - A_2\cos(\omega_2 t + \varphi_2)] \end{aligned} \tag{13}$$

As a result, if we can excite the masses so that $A_2 = 0$ then the masses will both oscillate at the frequency ω_1. In practice, we can do this by pulling the masses to the right by the same amount, so that $x_1(0) = \omega_2(0)$ which implies $A_2 = 0$. The solution is then $x_1 = x_2$ and both oscillate at the frequency A_1 for all time. This is the symmetric oscillation mode. Since $x_1 = x_2$ at all times, both masses move right together, then move left together.

On the other hand, if we excite the masses in such a way that $A_1 = 0$ then $x_1 = -x_2$ and both oscillate at frequency ω_2. We can set this up by pulling the masses in opposite directions. In this mode, when one mass is right of equilibrium, the other is left, and vice versa. So this is an antisymmetric mode.

It should be noticed that such a procedure is possible due to the simplicity of the analysed system.

From a general point of view, the problem to reduce the motion equations, which make reference to the system of a coupled oscillators, to formally simpler but physically equivalent expressions, which make reference to uncoupled oscillations, requires to perform a coordinate change in such a way to diagonalize the original equations so eliminating the mixed terms [40 - 43]. Of course, the new coordinates do not refer to the positions of the system real masses but each of them describes a collective property of the system, namely its normal modes. The utility of the diagonalization process is that, thanks to a coordinate change, the study of coupled oscillations reduces to the study of independent oscillations [44 - 48].

More specifically, a general method to find the motion solution for such a system, which is described by linear equations, is based on the matrix analysis of eigevalues and eigevectors.

Starting from eq.(3), we can write:

$$\begin{cases} m\ddot{x}_1 + 2kx_1 - kx_2 = 0 \\ m\ddot{x}_2 - kx_1 + 2kx_2 = 0 \end{cases} \quad (14)$$

and we can express these equations in a matrix form.

Let's consider:

$$\underline{u} = \begin{pmatrix} x_1 \\ x_2 \end{pmatrix} \quad (15)$$

and

$$\underline{\underline{k}} = \begin{pmatrix} 2k & -k \\ -k & 2k \end{pmatrix} \tag{16}$$

we obtain:

$$m\underline{\ddot{u}} + \underline{\underline{k}}\,\underline{u} = 0 \tag{17}$$

$$\underline{\ddot{u}} + \frac{\underline{\underline{k}}}{m}\underline{u} = 0 \tag{18}$$

We deal with homogeneous second order differential equations and to solve this kind of equation, we can consider the function test, *i.e.*:

$$\underline{u} = \underline{\underline{A}} e^{\lambda t} \tag{19}$$

$$\underline{\dot{u}} = \underline{\underline{A}} \lambda e^{\lambda t} \tag{20}$$

$$\underline{\ddot{u}} = \underline{\underline{A}} \lambda^2 e^{\lambda t} \tag{21}$$

Replacing in eq. (17), one gets:

$$\underline{\underline{A}} \lambda^2 e^{\lambda t} + \frac{\underline{\underline{k}}}{m} \underline{\underline{A}} e^{\lambda t} = 0 \tag{22}$$

$$\left(\lambda^2 \underline{\underline{I}} + \frac{\underline{\underline{k}}}{m} \right) = 0 \tag{23}$$

where $\underline{\underline{I}}$ is the identity matrix:

$$\underline{\underline{I}} = \begin{pmatrix} 1 & 0 \\ 0 & 1 \end{pmatrix} \qquad (24)$$

Substituting in (22):

$$\left[\lambda^2 \begin{pmatrix} 1 & 0 \\ 0 & 1 \end{pmatrix} + \frac{1}{m}\begin{pmatrix} 2k & -k \\ -k & 2k \end{pmatrix}\right] = 0 \qquad (25)$$

$$\left[\begin{pmatrix} \lambda^2 & 0 \\ 0 & \lambda^2 \end{pmatrix} + \frac{1}{m}\begin{pmatrix} \dfrac{2k}{m} & -\dfrac{k}{m} \\ -\dfrac{k}{m} & \dfrac{2k}{m} \end{pmatrix}\right] = 0 \qquad (26)$$

$$\begin{pmatrix} \lambda^2 + \dfrac{2k}{m} & -\dfrac{k}{m} \\ -\dfrac{k}{m} & \lambda^2 + \dfrac{2k}{m} \end{pmatrix} = 0 \qquad (27)$$

considering that $\omega = \sqrt{\dfrac{k}{m}}$ it is:

$$\begin{pmatrix} \lambda^2 + 2\omega^2 & -\omega^2 \\ -\omega^2 & \lambda^2 + 2\omega^2 \end{pmatrix} = 0 \qquad (28)$$

This is a 2x2 matrix that has two eigenvalues λ_i and two eigenvectors $\underline{u}_i$. To solve eq. (26) it must be imposed that the determinant of matrix is equal to zero:

$$0 = det\left(\lambda^2 \underline{I} + \omega^2\right) = det\begin{pmatrix} \lambda^2 + 2\omega^2 & -\omega^2 \\ -\omega^2 & \lambda^2 + 2\omega^2 \end{pmatrix}$$
$$= (\lambda^2 + 2\omega^2)^2 - (-\omega^2)^2 \tag{29}$$

This is a quadratic equation for λ^2, with two roots: the two eingevalues. Thus:

$$(\lambda^2 + 2\omega^2)^2 = (-\omega^2)^2 \tag{30}$$

$$(\lambda^2 + 2\omega^2)^2 = \mp(-\omega^2)^2 \tag{31}$$

$$\lambda^2 + 2\omega^2 = \mp(-\omega^2) \tag{32}$$

From this expression, the values of the two eingevalues are:

$$\lambda^2_1 = -2\omega^2 - \omega^2 = \mp 3\omega^2 \tag{33}$$

$$\lambda^2_2 = -2\omega^2 + \omega^2 = \mp\omega^2 \tag{34}$$

or in other words: $\omega_1 = \sqrt{\frac{k}{m}}$ and $\omega_2 = \sqrt{\frac{3k}{m}}$

These are the two normal mode frequencies we found above. Note that we didn't have to take the real part of the solution to find the normal mode frequencies. We only need to take the real part to find the solutions $x(t)$.

Again, it is interesting to note that for any initial condition one generates a motion which is a "composition" of the two normal motions [49 - 52]. The surprising aspect of the matter is that this motion is not periodic, that is, the system of the two masses, as far as we can wait, will never pass through a configuration already visited. This incredible property derives from the non-commensurability of the frequencies of the two normal modes (that is, from the impossibility of expressing their relationship through a rational number). In fact, we have:

EXPERIMENTAL SET-UP

The experimental set-up includes:

- Track for trolleys: it is a wood rod of 1 meter length, suitable for the hooking of fixed supports and for the sliding of the trolleys (Fig. **3a**).
- Fixed supports: screws of about 6 cm used to fix the springs.
- Trolleys: in wood, with plastic wheels, equipped with hooks on the front and rear to hook the springs. Each trolley is equipped with a plastic panel, fixed in the upper part, with the aim of ensuring that motion is detected by an ultrasonic sensor (Fig. **3b**).
- Ultrasonic sensor: it is a device capable of measuring the distance between itself and a specific object, in a range between 15 cm and 6 m, using ultrasound pulses; in addition to having a pulse emission system, it also capable of detecting the impulses that return to the detector after bouncing on the object. In this way, the detected ultrasound pulse is transformed into a vibration that excites the quartz proportionally to the recorded distance. The sensor, therefore, recording the time passed from the emission of the impulse to the reception, makes possible to calculate the distance at which the object is located as time changes. Finally, the recorded data, after being processed, is transmitted to the PC *via* an USB port to be analysed by the appropriate software.
- Springs set with a constant force of $k = 15$ N / m.
- Computer equipped with a Logger Lite data acquisition program.

Fig. (3). a) Trolley; **b)** ultrasonic sensor.

EXPERIMENTAL PROCEDURE

The supports are fixed to the track, at a distance of 0.7 m, and the springs are secured there and then connected to the hooks of the trolleys; finally, the two trolleys are connected by means of a third spring, as shown in Fig. (4).

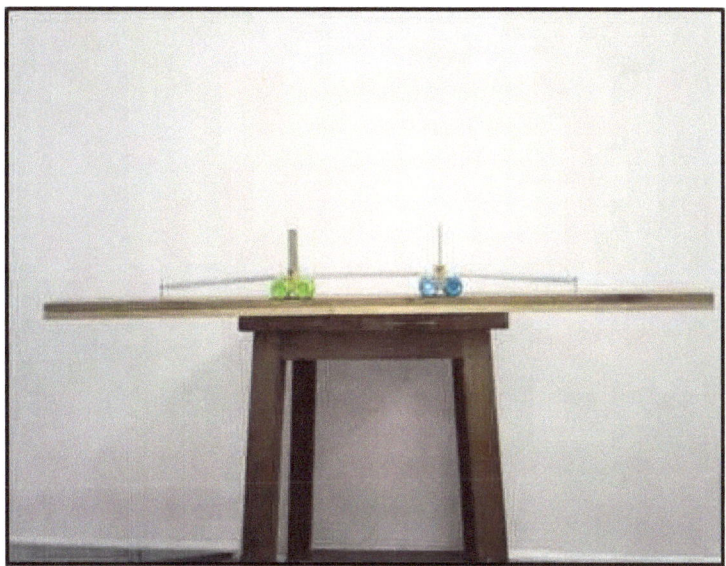

Fig. (4). Experimental set-up including two trolleys, three equal springs and a wood rod.

Particular attention was paid to securing the springs to the fixed support at the same height as the hook of the trolleys in order to minimize dissipation. Before starting the data acquisition, the position of the center of the trucks at rest on the track was registered. To record motion, the ultrasonic sensor was placed at the side, at the center and at the end of the experimental apparatus in such a way that the signal was at the same height. The data were then acquired, starting from the analysis of the normal mode conditions. In particular, we started by recording data in the case in which the trolleys moved in phase, moving them both from the equilibrium position in the same direction, by the same amount of space, and releasing them at the same time. Motion was recorded three times. Then we proceed with the case of the phase opposition, moving the trolleys them this time by the same amount of space from the equilibrium position, but in opposite directions. Again, three measurements were performed. We then continues with the acquisition of the data under different other conditions. From time to time the initial conditions of the experimental apparatus were registered and the measurement was performed. We proceeded until we reached a total of 10 different recorded motions.

Experimental Data

Fig. (**5**) shows, as an example, one displacement measurement acquired for the in phase condition, while (Fig. **6**) shows, as an example, one displacement measurement acquired for the out of phase condition.

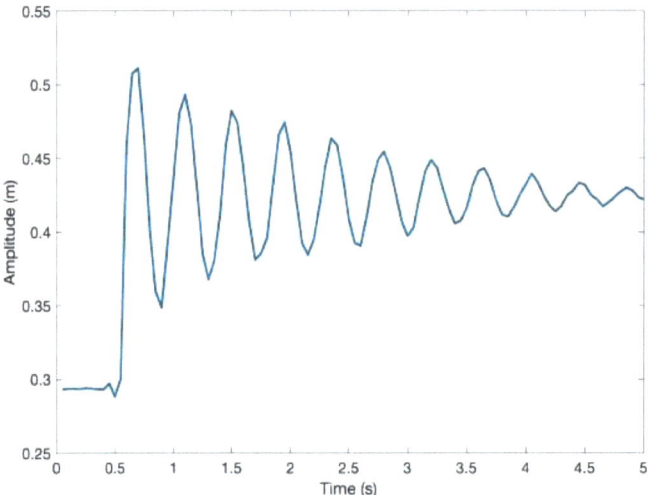

Fig. (5). Registered amplitude *versus* time for the in phase condition.

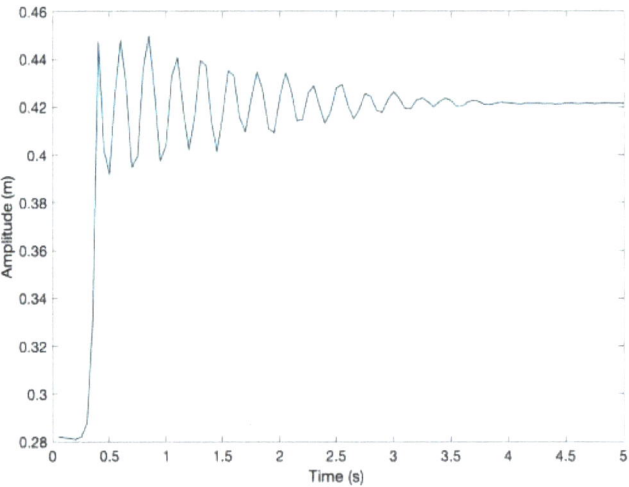

Fig. (6). Registered amplitude *versus* time for the out-of-phase condition.

Data Analysis

In our case we have that $\frac{\omega_2}{\omega_1} = \sqrt{3}$ where ω_2 is the angular velocity of the normal mode in phase, while ω_1 is the angular velocity of the normal mode in phase. Being:

$$\omega = \frac{2\pi}{T} \qquad (35)$$

we have that:

$$\frac{\omega_2}{\omega_1} = \frac{\frac{2\pi}{T_2}}{\frac{2\pi}{T_1}} = \frac{T_1}{T_2} \qquad (36)$$

where T_1 is the period of the in phase mode and T_2 is the period in the out of phase mode:

$$\frac{T_1}{T_2} = \frac{0,415}{0,236} = 1.75 \cong \sqrt{3} \qquad (37)$$

We proceeded with the data fitting process by using the damped. In particular, the function that describes the position of the body with respect to time is:

$$x(t) = A e^{-\tau t} \sin(\omega t + \varphi) + x_0 \qquad (38)$$

where ω is the angular velocity, φ the initial phase, A the amplitude constant and $e^{-\tau t}$ is a term which takes into account the dissipation of motion due to friction. To obtain the specific equation parameters for each normal mode, we proceeded as it follows:

- The time reference of the data was shifted so that the $t = 0$ condition corresponded to the first recorded minimum of the oscillatory motion.

- A quantity equal to 3/2 π was set as initial phase of motion, so that, for $t = 0$, the sine was equal to -1.
- The multiplicative constant A and the term x_0 were chosen so that, for $t = 0$, the value of the first minimum was obtained. So x_0 was equal to the average value of the oscillations, and A was to the deviation of the first minimum from it.

The obtained fitting equation of the normal phase mode, obtained following the method described above, is:

$$X_{1(t)} = 0{,}137 \cdot e^{-0{,}7 \cdot t} \cdot \sin\left(15{,}14 \cdot t + \frac{3}{2}\pi\right) + 0{,}425 \qquad (39)$$

The fitting result is reported in Fig. (7) where the fit curve is compared with the experimentally acquired set of measurements:

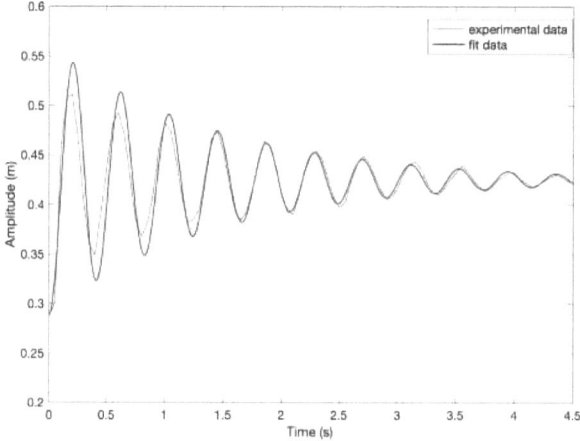

Fig. (7). Fit and experimental data of the in phase condition.

The obtained fitting equation of the normal phase mode in the out of phase condition is:

$$X_{2(t)} = 0{,}030 \cdot e^{-0{,}7 \cdot t} \cdot sin\left(26{,}62 \cdot t + \frac{3}{2}\pi\right) + 0{,}421 \qquad (40)$$

Fig. (8) reports the fitting result, where the fit curve is compared with the experimentally acquired set of measurements:

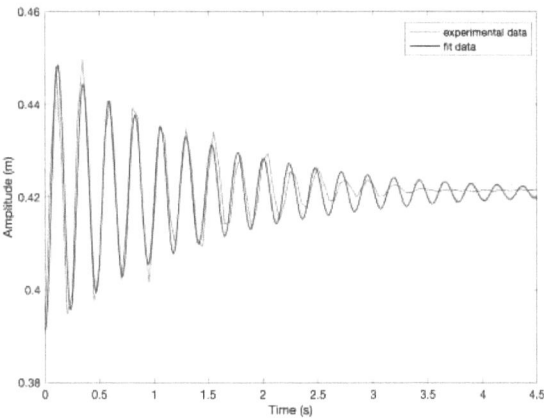

Fig. (8). Fit and experimental data of the out-of-phase condition.

HISTORICAL BACKGROUND: FOURIER AND WAVELET TRANSFORMS

Wavelet analysis appeared in the early 1980s mainly to fill the gaps in Fourier's analysis. This theory is a multidisciplinary work which brought together engineers, mathematicians and physicists who have developed similar ideas in their respective fields. The wavelet transform is similar to the Fourier transform. The main difference is that the Fourier theory is based on the fact that functions showing a certain degree of regularity can be represented by a linear combination of sines and cosines. The coefficients of this linear combination give information about the frequencies present in the signal. In general, the Fourier transform can be expressed with the following equation:

$$f(x) \sim \frac{a_0}{2} + \sum_{j=1}^{\infty}[a_j \cos(jx) + b_j \sin(jx)] \qquad (41)$$

where $f(x)$ is a periodic function defined for $0 \leq x \leq 2\pi$ a_0, a_j and b_j are the Fourier coefficients:

$$a_0 = \frac{1}{2\pi}\int_0^{2\pi} f(x)dx; \qquad (42)$$

$$a_j = \frac{1}{\pi}\int_0^{2\pi} f(x)dx \cos(jx); \qquad (43)$$

$$b_j = \frac{1}{\pi}\int_0^{2\pi} f(x)dx \sin(jx); \qquad (44)$$

More precisely, Fourier series are usually used to estimate the frequency spectrum of a given signal as a function of time. In medicine, for example, the electrocardiogram of a sick patient differs from that of a healthy patient. This difference, sometimes very difficult to spot when the electrocardiogram is given as a function of time, becomes evident when it is given as a function of frequencies, that is to say when looking at its Fourier coefficients. But the Fourier series give the amount of each frequency present in the signal for the entire observation period. The Fourier theory therefore becomes ineffective for a signal whose frequency spectrum varies considerably over time [52 - 57].

Furthermore, Fourier series are also used to approximate functions. Certain regular functions have an economic Fourier series, in other words they are well approximated with few Fourier coefficients. But since the sine and cosine functions have infinite support, the Fourier series does not work well when it has to locally describe a function which shows discontinuities. Thus, the Fourier transform of a given signal indicates how much of each frequency is in the signal but does not tell us when that time occurs. Instead, the wavelet transform offers the possibility of analysing a signal simultaneously in the time domain and in the frequency domain. Time-frequency information is necessary for a non-stationary signal (signal whose frequency content changes over time) but it is not necessary when the signal is stationary.

In other words, wavelet analysis consists in performing a local comparison of a signal in the manner of a mathematical microscope making it possible to zoom in on the signal at different scales. The transform executes a convolution between the signal and translates of a position p and dilates of a scale a of the mother wavelet to construct the two-dimensional field defined on the time-frequency plane (a, p).

$$W_\psi(a,p) = \frac{1}{\sqrt{a}} \int_{-\infty}^{+\infty} y(x)\psi^*\left(\frac{x-p}{a}\right) dx \qquad (45)$$

where a (positive) is the scale parameter, b is the shift (or position) parameter, symbol * denotes the complex conjugate and φ is a given function. This function can be chosen arbitrarily provided that it obeys certain rules, whose expression is:

$$\psi_{a,b} = \frac{1}{\sqrt{a}} \psi\left(\frac{x-p}{a}\right) \tag{46}$$

If the admissibility condition is satisfied, the transform is reversible and allows the signal to be reconstructed from the synthesis formula:

$$s(x) = \frac{1}{\sqrt{a}} \int_0^{+\infty} \int_{-\infty}^{+\infty} W_\psi(a,p) \psi\left(\frac{x-p}{a}\right) \frac{da\, dp}{a^2} \tag{47}$$

It is should be stressed that the translation and expansion (or dilatation) operations of a function in the physical space have their counterpart in the Fourier space. In order to better explain this behaviour, in the following figures three different cases are reported. More precisely, (Fig. 9) shows the translation of the function $\psi_p = \psi(x-p)$, by means of the position b and its Fourier Transform, $\mathcal{F}\psi_p(\omega) = e^{-i\omega p}\mathcal{F}(\omega)$. What it emerges is that, shifting the given function, the Fourier Transform is always the same.

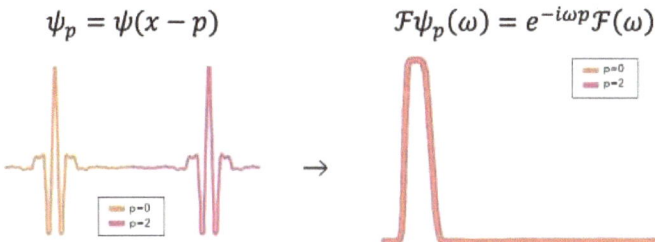

Fig. (9). Translation of the function $\psi_p = \psi(x-p)$, by means of the parameter p and its Fourier Transform, $\mathcal{F}\psi_p(\omega) = e^{-i\omega p}\mathcal{F}(\omega)$. By shifting the given function, the Fourier Transform is always the same.

(Fig. 10) reports the dilatation and the contraction of the function $\psi_a = \psi(ax)$, by means of the scale parameter a, with their Fourier Transform.

$$\mathcal{F}\psi_a(\omega) = \frac{1}{|a|} \mathcal{F}\left(\frac{\omega}{a}\right) \tag{48}$$

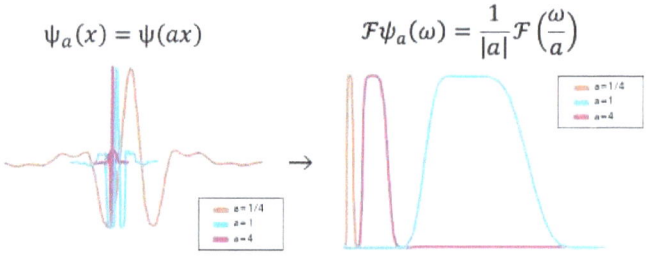

Fig. (10). Dilatation and contraction of the function $\psi_a = \psi(ax)$ by means of the scale parameter a, with their Fourier Transform, $\mathcal{F}\psi_a(\omega) = \frac{1}{|a|}\mathcal{F}\left(\frac{\omega}{a}\right)$ The amplitude of the FT contracts when the function expands and widens when the function contracts.

As it can be seen, the amplitude of the FT contracts when the function expands and widens when the function contracts.

Finally, in Fig. **(11)** a combination of translation and dilatation of the given function by means of *(a, p)* is presented. In particular, on the left, three different functions obtained varying the value of *a* and *b* $\psi_{a,b} = \frac{1}{\sqrt{a}}\psi\left(\frac{x-p}{a}\right)$ of are reported and on the right the Fourier Transform, of each function obtained. In this case the amplitude and the height of the Fourier Transform changes by varying the two parameters *(a, p)*.

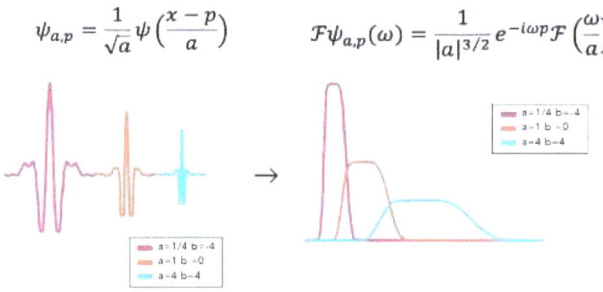

Fig. (11). Combination of translation and dilatation of the given function by means of *(a, p)*. On the left, three different functions obtained varying the value of *a* and *p* of $\psi_{a,p} = \frac{1}{\sqrt{a}}\psi\left(\frac{x-p}{a}\right)$ and on the right the Fourier Transform, of each function obtained. The amplitude and the height of the Fourier Transform changes by varying the two parameters *(a, p)*.

In summary, the representation of the translated-dilatated behaviour of the wavelet in the time-frequency plane is reported in Fig. **(12)**.

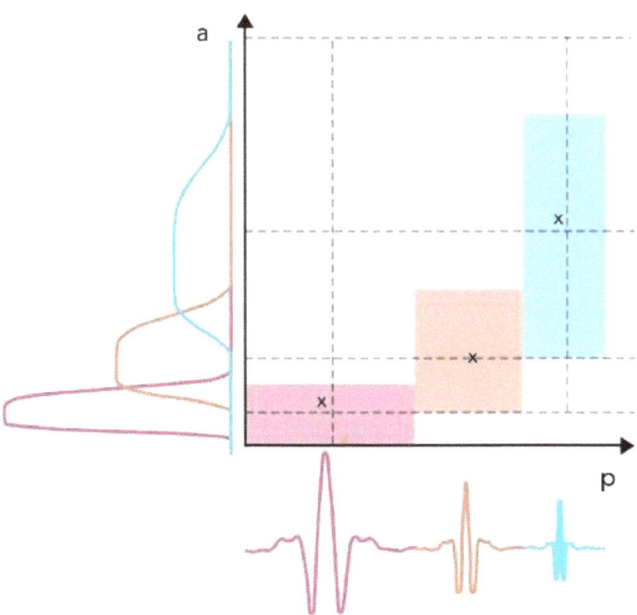

Fig. (12). Representation of the translated-dilatated behaviour of the wavelet in the time-frequency plane.

By choosing suitable couples *(a, p)* it is possible to cover all the whole time-frequency plane. This property gives rise to an analogy with the optical microscope which allows to zoom inside the signal at a position given by the focal length a, with a enlargement given proportional to $1/a$ and the objective of the microscope given by the choice by the wavelet [58 - 63].

The choice of the wavelet used for the time-frequency decomposition is the most important point. This has an influence on the time and frequency resolution of the result [64, 65].

It is well known that the low frequencies have a good frequency resolution but a bad temporal resolution while the high frequencies have a good temporal resolution and a bad frequency resolution.

In such a way, we cannot modify the characteristics of the wavelet transform, but we can however increase the total frequency resolution or total time resolution. This is directly proportional to the width of the wavelet used in real space and in Fourier space. For our study, we have chosen the Morlet wavelet because it is very localized from the point of view of frequencies. As it can be seen, the wavelet transform is in fact an infinite set of various transforms, depending on the function used to calculate it. This is the reason why the wavelet transform is treated in very diverse contexts and applications. Furthermore, correct frequency localization of the wavelet is essential in order not to diffuse the energy of the analysis over multiple frequency bands. It should however be noted that the fact of contracting a wavelet to gain precision in time is done at the price of a spread in frequency behind which hides the principle of uncertainty of Heisenberg. It becomes possible to visualize the wavelet energy of a given signal by adopting the scalogram representation which consists in drawing the isocontour lines of the module of the wavelet field calculated on the dyadic network [66 - 70].

APPLICATION OF FOURIER AND WAVELET TRANSFORMS

In order to explain how WT works and the advantages of this method in respect to FT, a comparison between the two transforms has been performed. In particular, (Fig. 13) reports on the top the measurement acquired for the in phase condition and on the bottom, at left the WT scalogram and on the right the FT. What it emerges is that while FT furnishes only a value of the motion average frequency at 2.38 Hz, WT allows to simultaneously execute a time–frequency analysis and indicates how much time the motion average frequency spreads over time.

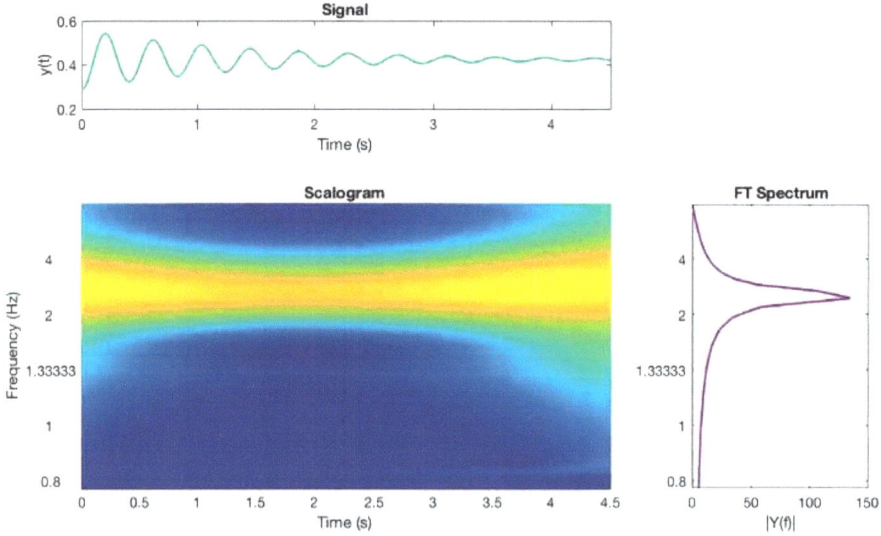

Fig. (13). Comparison between FT and WT for the in phase condition. On the top the in phase amplitude *versus* time. On the bottom, at left the WT scalogram and on the right the FT. What it emerges is that while FT furnishes only a value of the motion average frequency at 2.38 Hz, WT allows to simultaneously execute a time–frequency analysis.

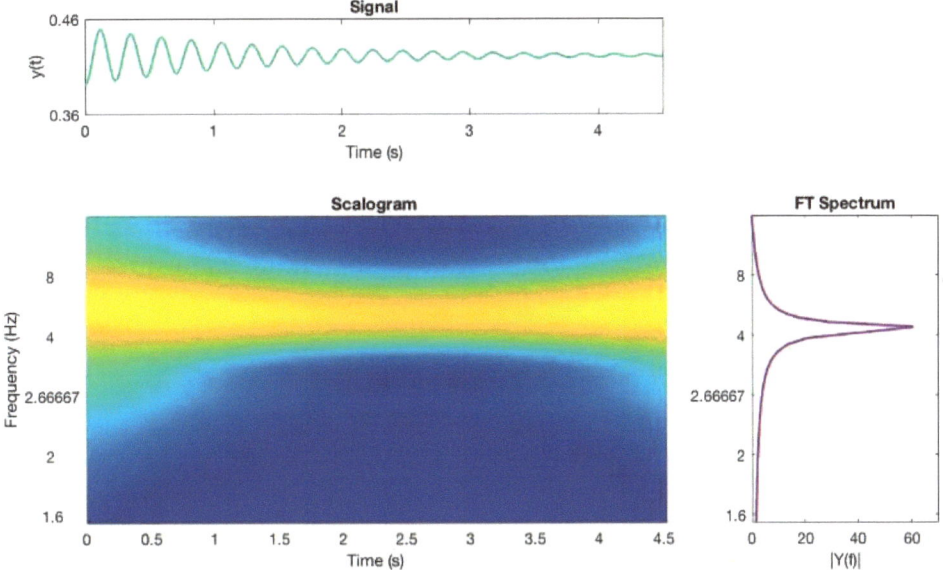

Fig. (14). Comparison between FT and WT for the out phase condition. On the top the out of phase amplitude *versus* time and on the bottom, at left the WT scalogram and on the right the FT. As it can be seen FT furnishes only a value of the motion average frequency at 4.12 Hz while WT allows to simultaneously execute a time–frequency analysis.

(Fig. **14**) shows on the top the measurement acquired for the out of phase condition and on the bottom, at left the WT scalogram and on the right the FT. As it can be seen, FT provides a value of the motion average frequency at 4.12 Hz and WT allows to simultaneously execute a time–frequency analysis and indicates how much time the motion average frequency spreads over time.

From this analysis emerges that the frequency for the in phase condition, ω_1, is equal to 2.38 Hz while that the frequency for the out phase condition, ω_2, is 4.12Hz. Their ratio is just $\sqrt{3}$. Both the procedures confirm that $\omega_2 = \sqrt{3}\omega_1$.

CONCLUDING REMARKS

The present work reports the contents of an academic lecture on a system of coupled oscillators. The physical system constituted by two oscillating masses interacting through a connecting spring is studied. The theory that describes the system dynamics is presented following two different procedures. In particular, on that score, the matrix diagonalization process has been introduced; it is shown how this approach allows to reduce the coupled oscillation equations to equivalent equations which refer to uncoupled oscillations. However, the coordinates, which diagonalize the matrix associated to the motion equation system, do not refer to the positions of the real masses but describe collective properties of the system, namely its normal modes. In order to improve the understanding of the adopted analytical procedure, an experiment addressed to evaluate the frequencies of the system normal modes is proposed. On that score, for analysing the oscillation amplitude as a function of time, a comparison between Fourier Transform and Wavelet Transform is presented. What it emerges is that, differently from what occurs for Fourier Transform which provides a value of the motion average frequency, the Wavelet Transform allows to simultaneously execute a time–frequency analysis.

CONSENT FOR PUBLICATION

Not applicable.

CONFLICT OF INTEREST

The authors declare no conflict of interest, financial or otherwise.

ACKNOWLEDGEMENTS

Declared none.

REFERENCES

[1] R. Trumper, "The Physics Laboratory – A Historical Overview and Future Perspectives", *Sci. Educ.,* vol. 12, pp. 645-670, 2003.
[http://dx.doi.org/10.1023/A:1025692409001]

[2] R. Khaparde, "What are the objectives and goals of physics laboratory courses? A survey of college teachers", *J. Phys. Conf. Ser.,* vol. 1286, no. 1, p. 012037, 2019.
[http://dx.doi.org/10.1088/1742-6596/1286/1/012037]

[3] G. Andaloro, L. Bellamonte, and R. Sperandeo-Mineo, "A Computer-Based Learning Environment in the Field of Newtonian Mechanics", *Int. J. Sci. Educ.,* vol. 19, pp. 661-680, 1997.
[http://dx.doi.org/10.1080/0950069970190604]

[4] A. Arons, "Achieving Wider Scientific Literacy", *Daedalus,* vol. 112, pp. 91-122, 1983.

[5] A. Arons, "Guiding Insight and Inquiry in the Introductory Physics Laboratory", *Phys. Teach.,* vol. 31, pp. 278-282, 1993.
[http://dx.doi.org/10.1119/1.2343763]

[6] H. Brasell, "The Effect of Real-Time Laboratory Graphing on Learning Graphic Representation of Distance and Velocity", *J. Res. Sci. Teach.,* vol. 24, pp. 385-395, 1987.
[http://dx.doi.org/10.1002/tea.3660240409]

[7] G. Calverley, D. Finchman, and D. Bacon, "Modernisation of a Traditional Physics Course", *Comp. Educ.,* vol. 31, pp. 151-169, 1998.
[http://dx.doi.org/10.1016/S0360-1315(98)00018-9]

[8] M. Crosby, "M.; Iding, The Influence of a Multimedia Physics Tutor and User Differences on the Development of Scientific Knowledge", *Comp. Educ.,* vol. 29, pp. 127-136, 1997.
[http://dx.doi.org/10.1016/S0360-1315(97)00024-9]

[9] R. Driver, H. Asoko, J. Leach, E. Mortimer, and P. Scott, "Constructing Scientific Knowledge in the Classroom", *Educ. Res.,* vol. 23, pp. 5-12, 1994.
[http://dx.doi.org/10.3102/0013189X023007005]

[10] D. Dykstra, F. Boyle, and I. Monarch, "Studying Conceptual Change in Learning Physics", *Sci. Educ.,* vol. 76, pp. 615-652, 1992.
[http://dx.doi.org/10.1002/sce.3730760605]

[11] B. Eylon, M. Ronen, and U. Ganiel, "Computer Simulations as Tools for Teaching and Learning: Using a Simulation Environment in Optics", *J. Sci. Educ. Technol.,* vol. 5, pp. 93-110, 1996.
[http://dx.doi.org/10.1007/BF01575150]

[12] Y. Friedler, R. Nachmias, and M. Linn, "Learning Scientific Reasoning Skills in Microcomputer-Based Laboratories", *J. Res. Sci. Teach.,* vol. 27, pp. 173-191, 1990.
[http://dx.doi.org/10.1002/tea.3660270208]

[13] J. Gilbert, R. Osborne, and P. Fensham, "Children's Science and its Consequences for Teaching", *Sci. Educ.,* vol. 66, pp. 623-633, 1982.
[http://dx.doi.org/10.1002/sce.3730660412]

[14] R. Hake, "Socratic Pedagogy in the Introductory Physics Laboratory", *Phys. Teach.,* vol. 30, pp. 546-552, 1982.
[http://dx.doi.org/10.1119/1.2343637]

[15] M. Krieger, and J. Stith, "Spreadsheets in the Physics Laboratory", *Phys. Teach.,* vol. 28, pp. 378-384, 1990.
[http://dx.doi.org/10.1119/1.2343079]

[16] K. Kumpulainen, and M. Mutanen, "Collaborative Practice of Science Construction in a Computer-Based Multimedia Environment", *Comp. Educ.,* vol. 30, pp. 75-85, 1998.
[http://dx.doi.org/10.1016/S0360-1315(97)00082-1]

[17] P.W. Laws, "Millikan Lecture 1996: Promoting Active Learning Based on Physics Education Research in Introductory Physics Courses", *Am. J. Phys.,* vol. 65, pp. 14-21, 1998.
[http://dx.doi.org/10.1119/1.18496]

[18] P. Laws, "Calculus-Based Physics without Lectures", *Phys. Today,* vol. 44, pp. 24-31, 1991.
[http://dx.doi.org/10.1063/1.881276]

[19] A. Lawson, "How Do Humans Acquire Knowledge? And What Does That Imply about the Nature of Knowledge", *Sci. Educ.,* vol. 9, pp. 577-598, 2000.
[http://dx.doi.org/10.1023/A:1008756715517]

[20] D. Maor, and P. Taylor, "Teacher Epistemology and Scientific Inquiry in Computerized Classroom Environments", *J. Res. Sci. Teach.,* vol. 32, pp. 839-854, 1995.
[http://dx.doi.org/10.1002/tea.3660320807]

[21] L. Mason, "An Analysis of Children's Construction of New Knowledge through Their Use of Reasoning and Arguing in Classroom Discussions", *Int. J. Qual. Stud. Educ.,* vol. 9, pp. 411-433, 1996.
[http://dx.doi.org/10.1080/0951839960090404]

[22] M. Matthews, "M. "History, Philosophy, and Science Teaching: A Reapprochement", *Stud. Sci. Educ.,* vol. 18, pp. 25-51, 1990.
[http://dx.doi.org/10.1080/03057269008559980]

[23] M. Matthews, "Introductory Comments on Philosophy and Constructivism in Science Education", *Sci. Educ.,* vol. 6, pp. 5-14, 1997.
[http://dx.doi.org/10.1023/A:1008650823980]

[24] R. Millar, 2What is Scientific Method and Can it be Taught?*Skills and Processes in Science Education.,* J. Wellington, Ed., Routledge: London, 1989.

[25] R. Nachmias, and M. Linn, "Evaluation of Science Laboratory Data: The Role of Computer-Presented Information", *J. Res. Sci. Teach.,* vol. 24, pp. 491-506, 1987.
[http://dx.doi.org/10.1002/tea.3660240509]

[26] M. Sifuzzaman, M.R. Islam, and M.Z. Ali, "Application of Wavelet Transform and its Advantages Compared to Fourier Transform", *J. Physiol. Sci.,* vol. 13, pp. 121-134, 2009.

[27] M.T. Caccamo, V. Zammuto, C. Gugliandolo, C. Madeleine-Perdrillat, A. Spanò, and S. Magazù, "Thermal restraint of a bacterial exopolysaccharide of shallow vent origin", *Int. J. Biol. Macromol.,* vol. 114, pp. 649-655, 2018.
[http://dx.doi.org/10.1016/j.ijbiomac.2018.03.160] [PMID: 29601879]

[28] L. Debnat, ""Wavelet Transforms and Their Applications", Proc. Nat. Acad. Sci", *India Section A: Phys. Sci.,* vol. 6, pp. 685-690, 1998.

[29] M.T. Caccamo, and S. Magazù, "Ethylene Glycol - Polyethylene Glycol (EG-PEG) Mixtures: Infrared Spectra Wavelet Cross-Correlation Analysis", *Appl. Spectrosc.,* vol. 71, no. 3, pp. 401-409, 2017.
[http://dx.doi.org/10.1177/0003702816662882] [PMID: 27558367]

[30] O. Rioul, and M. Vetterli, "Wavelets and Signal Processing", *Signal Proc. Mag,* vol. 8, pp. 14-38, 1991.
[http://dx.doi.org/10.1109/79.91217]

[31] A. Cannuli, M.T. Caccamo, G. Castorina, F. Colombo, and S. Magazù, "Laser Techniques on Acoustically Levitated Droplets", *EPJ Web Conf.,* vol. 167, 2018 art. n. 05010.

[32] M.S. Tiersten, "Force, Momentum Change, and Motion", *Am. Ass. Phys. Teach,* vol. 37, pp. 82-87, 1969.

[33] R. Plastino, and J.C. Muzzio, "On the use and abuse of Newton's second law for variable mass problems", *Celestial Mech. Dyn. Astron.,* vol. 53, pp. 227-232, 1992.
[http://dx.doi.org/10.1007/BF00052611]

[34] R. Feynman, R.B. Leighton, and M. Sands, *The Feynman Lectures on Physics.* vol. 1. Addison-Wesley, 1964.

[35] Z. Sun, "Normal Mode Splitting in a Moving-Particles-Pumped Mechanical Oscillator: Clamped-Hinged Homogeneous Beam", *Sci. Rep.,* vol. 8, no. 1, p. 9803, 2018.
[http://dx.doi.org/10.1038/s41598-018-27989-8] [PMID: 29955100]

[36] G.V. Rao, "Linear dynamics of an elastic beam under moving loads", *J. Vib. Acoust.,* vol. 122, pp. 281-289, 2000.
[http://dx.doi.org/10.1115/1.1303822]

[37] H. Ouyang, "H. Moving-load dynamic problems: A tutorial", *Mech. Syst. Signal Process.,* vol. 25, pp. 2039-2060, 2011.
[http://dx.doi.org/10.1016/j.ymssp.2010.12.010]

[38] R.J. Thompson, G. Rempe, and H.J. Kimble, "Observation of normal-mode splitting for an atom in an optical cavity", *Phys. Rev. Lett.,* vol. 68, no. 8, pp. 1132-1135, 1992.
[http://dx.doi.org/10.1103/PhysRevLett.68.1132] [PMID: 10046088]

[39] J.M. Dobrindt, I. Wilson-Rae, and T.J. Kippenberg, "Parametric normal-mode splitting in cavity optomechanics", *Phys. Rev. Lett.,* vol. 101, no. 26, p. 263602, 2008.
[http://dx.doi.org/10.1103/PhysRevLett.101.263602] [PMID: 19113771]

[40] S. Huang, and G.S. Agarwal, "Normal-mode splitting in a coupled system of a nanomechanical oscillator and a parametric amplifier cavity", *Phys. Rev. A,* vol. 80, p. 033807, 2009.
[http://dx.doi.org/10.1103/PhysRevA.80.033807]

[41] S.A.Q. Siddiqui, M.F. Golnaraghi, and G.R. Heppler, "Dynamics of a flexible beam carrying a moving mass using perturbation, numerical and time-frequency analysis techniques", *J. Sound Vibrat.,* vol. 229, pp. 1023-1055, 2000.

[http://dx.doi.org/10.1006/jsvi.1999.2449]

[42] S. Park, and Y. Youm, "Motion of a moving elastic beam carrying a moving mass - analysis and experimental verification", *J. Sound Vibrat.,* vol. 240, pp. 131-157, 2001.
[http://dx.doi.org/10.1006/jsvi.2000.3198]

[43] A.H. Nayfeh, and D.T. Mook, *Nonlinear Oscillations (Wiley Classics Library Edition)* vol. 5. Wiley Interscience: New York, 1995, pp. 258-364.

[44] S. Huang, and G.S. Agarwal, "2Normal-mode splitting in a coupled system of a nanomechanical oscillator and a parametric amplifier cavity", *Phys. Rev. A,* vol. 80, p. 033807, 2009.
[http://dx.doi.org/10.1103/PhysRevA.80.033807]

[45] S. Belbasi, "Anti-resonance in a one-dimensional chain of driven coupled oscillators", *Am. J. Phys.,* vol. 82, p. 32, 2014.
[http://dx.doi.org/10.1119/1.4827277]

[46] J.B. Marion, and S.T. Thornton, *Classical Dynamics of Particles and Systems.* 3rd ed. Harcourt Brace Jovanovich, 1988.

[47] H.J. Pain, *The Physics of Vibrations and Waves.* 6th ed. Wiley: Chichester, 2005.
[http://dx.doi.org/10.1002/0470016957]

[48] M.E. Foulaadvand, and D. Masoumi, "Mechanical filtering in forced-oscillation of two coupled pendulums", *Phys. Educ.,* vol. 27, pp. 39-51, 2010.

[49] R. Givens, O.F. de Alcantara Bonfim, and R.B. Ormond, "Direct observation of normal modes in coupled oscillators", *Am. J. Phys.,* vol. 71, pp. 87-90, 2003.
[http://dx.doi.org/10.1119/1.1519230]

[50] J.A. Monsoriu, M.H. Giménez, J. Riera, and A. Vidaurre, "Measuring coupled oscillations using an automated video analysis technique based on image recognition", *Eur. J. Phys.,* vol. 26, pp. 1149-1155, 2005.
[http://dx.doi.org/10.1088/0143-0807/26/6/023]

[51] M. Giménez, J. Castro Palacio, J. Gómez-Tejedor, L. Velazquez, and J. Monsoriu, "Theoretical and experimental study of the normal modes in a coupled two-dimensional system", *Rev. Mexi. Fis. E.,* vol. Vol. 63, 2016.

[52] R. Givens, O. Bonfim, and R. Ormond, "Direct observation of normal modes in coupled oscillators", *Amer. J. Phys,* vol. 71, 2003.
[http://dx.doi.org/10.1119/1.1519230]

[53] M.T. Caccamo, A. Cannuli, and S. Magazù, "Wavelet analysis of near-resonant series RLC circuit with time-dependent forcing frequency", *Eur. J. Phys.,* vol. 39, p. aaae77, 2018.
[http://dx.doi.org/10.1088/1361-6404/aaae77]

[54] M.T. Caccamo, and S. Magazù, Conic Pendulum of Variable Length Analysed by wavelets.*New Trends in Physics Education Research* Nova Science Publishers, Inc., 2018, pp. 117-131.

[55] M.T. Caccamo, and S. Magazù, "Variable Length Pendulum Analyzed by a Comparative Fourier and Wavelet Approach", *Rev. Mex. Fis. E,* vol. 64, pp. 81-86, 2018.
[http://dx.doi.org/10.31349/RevMexFisE.64.81]

[56] M.T. Caccamo, G. Castorina, F. Catalano, and S. Magazù, "Rüchardt's experiment treated by Fourier transform", *Eur. J. Phys.,* vol. 40, p. 02570, 2019.
[http://dx.doi.org/10.1088/1361-6404/aaf66c]

[57] S. Magazù, and M.T. Caccamo, Fourier and wavelet Analyses of Climate Data.*New Trends in Physics Education Research* Nova Science Publishers, Inc., 2018, pp. 226-241.

[58] H. Adeli, Z. Zhou, and N. Dadmehr, "Analysis of EEG records in an epileptic patient using wavelet transform", *J. Neurosci. Methods,* vol. 123, no. 1, pp. 69-87, 2003.
[http://dx.doi.org/10.1016/S0165-0270(02)00340-0] [PMID: 12581851]

[59] S. Magazù, F. Migliardo, and M.T. Caccamo, "Innovative wavelet protocols in analyzing elastic incoherent neutron scattering", *J. Phys. Chem. B,* vol. 116, no. 31, pp. 9417-9423, 2012.
[http://dx.doi.org/10.1021/jp3060087] [PMID: 22793379]

[60] S. Magazù, F. Migliardo, B.G. Vertessy, and M.T. Caccamo, "Investigations of Homologous Disaccharides by Elastic Incoherent Neutron Scattering and Wavelet Multiresolution Analysis", *Chem. Phys.,* vol. 424, pp. 56-61, 2013.
[http://dx.doi.org/10.1016/j.chemphys.2013.05.004]

[61] J.B. Ramsey, "Wavelets in Economics and Finance: Past and Future", *Stud. Nonlinear Dyn. Econom.,* vol. 6, pp. 1-27, 2002.
[http://dx.doi.org/10.2202/1558-3708.1090]

[62] F. Migliardo, M.T. Caccamo, and S. Magazù, "Elastic Incoherent Neutron Scatterings Wavevector and Thermal Analysis on Glass-forming Homologous Disaccharides", *J. Non-Cryst. Solids,* vol. 378, pp. 144-151, 2013.
[http://dx.doi.org/10.1016/j.jnoncrysol.2013.06.030]

[63] M.T. Caccamo, and S. Magazù, "Multiscaling Wavelet Analysis of Infrared and Raman Data on Polyethylene Glycol 1000 Aqueous Solutions", *Spectrosc. Lett.,* vol. 50, pp. 130-136, 2017.
[http://dx.doi.org/10.1080/00387010.2017.1291524]

[64] X.G. Miao, and W. Moon, "Application of wavelet transform in reflection seismic data analysis", *Geosci. J.,* vol. 3, pp. 171-179, 1999.
[http://dx.doi.org/10.1007/BF02910273]

[65] N. Ahuja, S. Lertrattanapanich, and N.K. Bose, "Properties determining choice of mother wavelet", *IEEE Proc. – Vis. Image Signal Proc,* vol. 152, 2005no. 5, pp. 659-664
[http://dx.doi.org/10.1049/ip-vis:20045034]

[66] J. Morlet, G. Arens, E. Fourgeau, and D. Glard, "Wave propagation and sampling theory; Part I, Complex signal and scattering in multilayered media", *Geophys.,* vol. 47, pp. 203-221, 1982.
[http://dx.doi.org/10.1190/1.1441328]

[67] M.T. Caccamo, and S. Magazù, "Variable mass pendulum behaviour processed by wavelet analysis", *Eur. J. Phys.,* vol. 38, p. 015804, 2017.
[http://dx.doi.org/10.1088/0143-0807/38/1/015804]

[68] I. Daubechies, "The Wavelet Transform, Time-Frequency Localization and Signal Analysis", *IEEE Trans. Inf. Theory,* vol. 36, pp. 961-1005, 1990.
[http://dx.doi.org/10.1109/18.57199]

[69] A.W. Galli, G.T. Heydt, and P.F. Ribeiro, "Exploring the power of wavelet analysis", *IEEE Comput. Appl. Power,* vol. 9, pp. 37-41, 1996.
[http://dx.doi.org/10.1109/67.539845]

[70] F. Colombo, M.T. Caccamo, and S. Magazù, Wavelet analysis as a tool for characterizing trends in climatic data.*Wavelets: Principles, Analysis and Applications (Book Chapter)* Nova Science Publishers, Inc., 2018, pp. 55-76.

SUBJECT INDEX

A

Abilities 1, 13, 15, 17, 20, 32, 33
   cognitive 17
   creative 15, 20
   mathematical 20
Account flame tests 76
Active learning 14, 22, 74
   methods 14, 22
   strategies 74
Activities 14, 16, 20, 41, 42, 77, 83
   active-learning 14, 16
   engineering 14
   experimental 77, 83
   inter-student 41
   monologic 42
   project 16, 20
Aerodynamic regimes, well-defined 35
Aggregated web activities 42
Amplitude 87, 99, 104, 108
   constant 99
   oscillation 87, 108
Angular velocity 99
Antagonistic 41, 66
   actors/stakeholders 66
   understandings 41
Applications 5, 6, 15, 24 29, 42, 106
   biological 6
   biomedical 5, 6
   energetic 24
Approach 37, 41, 42, 49, 88
   critical 42
   integrated 88
   pedagogic 49
   post-development 41
   progressive 37
Artificial intelligence 21
Assessment 21, 25, 31
   competence 31
   mutual 21
Atomic energy levels 81
Atoms 80, 82, 84
   hydrogen 82, 84
   ionized helium 80
Authentic entrepreneurship 54

B

Balance, argumentative 27, 32
Balmer 76, 78
   Rydberg's formula 78
   series 76
Balmer's 76, 78
   coefficients 76
   formula 78
Bernoulli's principle 5
Black body emission formalism 78
Blocks, designed building 35
Blood pressure 5, 6
   activities 6
   cuff 5
   lab activity 5
Bohr 77, 81
   model 77
   orbit model 81
Bohr's model 78
Border conditions, social 35
Boundary conditions result 37

C

Canadian product WebCT 66
Cardiovascular system 2
Careers 2, 4, 5, 64
   health science 5
   professional 64
Civil 29, 54
   engineering 65
   society 29
Class 1, 2, 3, 4, 6, 17, 29, 68
   introductory physics laboratory 1
Climate change and climate models 65
Climate models 65
Coefficients 17, 20, 21, 76, 78, 101

correlation 20, 21
surface tension 17
Cognitive activity 13, 14
Cohorts, young 24
College, technical 65
Combustion 33, 36, 37
  chamber 33
  engine, internal 36
Communication 21, 26, 29, 32, 42
  international scientific 21
  media 32
Community 3, 21, 41
  international scientific student 21
  learning technologies 41
Comparison of joint features 37
Competence 22, 32
  communicative 32
  organizational 32
  professional 32
Complexities 13, 15, 16, 24, 42, 50, 52, 53, 54
  academic 50
  iterative 24
  of cultural diversity 42
  social 52, 53, 54
Concept-based labs 4
Conceptual 4, 77, 82
  laboratory 77
  physics 4
  referents, fundamental 82
Concrete didactic process 26
Conditions 2, 36, 37, 103
  admissibility 103
  boundary 36, 37
  experimental 2
Connections 1, 2, 3, 4, 5, 6, 7, 9, 14, 15, 17, 29, 32, 72, 73, 88
  explicit 7
  interdisciplinary 6, 14, 29, 32
  logical 17
  oscillating 88
  temporal 3
Consensual conferences 64
Consensus 25, 32, 50, 64, 65, 68
  complex 68
  constructed 50
  constructing 68
  equlilibrating 68
Coupled oscillators 87, 89, 92, 107
Courses 1, 3, 7, 8, 25, 33, 64, 65
  implementing introductory college physics laboratory 1
  variable interdisciplinary 64
Creative assignments 19
Crystallization nuclei 29
Cultural competencies, general 14
Cultures, science-based humanitarian 49

D

Data 79, 99
  analysis 79, 99
  interpretation 79
DBR 78, 79, 83
  methodologies 78, 79
  methods 83
Degree of freedom 35
Design 1, 3, 8, 16, 17, 34, 35, 36, 37, 49, 50, 72, 73, 74, 75
  based research (DBR) 72, 74
  dialogic 35
  engineering 16
  graphic 49, 50
  mechanical 35
  social 36
  technological 17
Development 3, 13, 14, 15, 16, 21, 22, 33, 40, 41, 74
  global 40
  historical 74
  intensive 15
Developmental paradigms 41
Devices 7, 14, 16, 17, 18, 19, 96
  electrostatic 19
  physical 17
Didactic 26, 33, 44, 51, 55, 66, 68, 88
  functionality 66
  goals 51
  itinerary, significant 88
  procedures 33, 44

concrete 26, 68
  program, elaborated 55
Diffraction 5, 6, 75, 76, 77
  pattern 75, 76
  spectrometer 5, 6
  toy glasses 77
Discourse 42, 64
  activities 42
  ethics 64
Doppler's effect 21
DPSIR concept 32
Dyadic network 106
Dynamic inter-students communication patterns 65

E

Education 3, 13, 14, 15, 16, 21, 22, 37, 54, 68
  college 3
  contemporary 54
  engineering 14
  general 14
  modern 21
Educational 14, 15, 17, 22, 72, 74, 77, 79, 83
  material 15
  path 72, 74, 77, 79, 83
  process 14, 15, 17, 22
Educational activities 13, 16
  problem-oriented 16
Effects 32, 76
  greenhouse 32
  photoelectric 76
EKG 6
  activity 6
  lab activity 6
e-learning 26, 33, 38, 41, 42, 43
Electromagnetic induction 16
Emission(s) 32, 72, 76, 77, 78, 79, 81, 82, 83, 96
  discrete 83
  luminous 76
  spectra 79
Emitted 76, 82
  light pattern 76

  photons 82
Empirical dimension 87
Energy 16, 17, 54, 73, 74, 75, 76, 77, 78, 79, 82, 106
  electric 54
  emitted 82
  mechanical 16
  potential 17
  radiant 74
Energy levels 73, 77, 80, 82, 83
  first five 80
  single 82
Energy nature 77
Environment 21, 22, 33, 40, 42, 65
  comfortable psychological learning 22
  enhanced learning 40
  multicultural 42
  networked 65
Environmental 27, 30, 32, 65
  effects 65
  protection 32
  systems sciences 27, 30, 65
  technology 65
Environmental impact assessment (EIA) 54, 57
  directive 54
Equations 35, 87, 90, 91, 92, 93, 95, 101, 107
  coupled oscillation 87, 107
  differential 35, 93
  linear 92
  quadratic 95
Ethical measurement systems 54

F

Fact-based arguments, specialised 68
Flame tests 76
Foreign language section 21
Fourier 87, 89, 101, 102, 103, 104, 108
  coefficients 101, 102
  series 102
  theory 101, 102
  Transform 87, 89, 101, 102, 103, 104, 108
Four-stroke cycle engine 36

Framework 20, 40, 41, 73, 74, 83, 88
  theoretical 74, 83
Frequency 87, 89, 102, 106, 107, 108
  analysis 87, 89, 106, 107, 108
  bands, multiple 106
  domain 102
  localization, correct 106
Frequency resolution 105
  bad 105
  total 105
Fürstenfeld highway 65

G

Game 68, 69
  based learning tradition 68
  web-based negotiation 69
Gas 35, 79, 81
  discharge lamp 79
  emitting 81
  particles 35
  stream 35
Generator 18, 19
  electrostatic 18
Graaff's 18
  electrostatic generator 18
  model 18
Graduate student 1, 4, 7
  instructors 1
  teaching assistants 4, 7

H

Harmonic oscillator 91
Heat engines 19
Hooke's law 89

I

Industrial electronics 65
Inquiry-based learning strategies 72
Interdisciplinary 1, 3, 20, 25, 28, 29, 31, 33, 39
  collaboration 25

cooperation 28
education 3
goal 1
internships 33
project work 20
Inter-paradigmatic approach 25
Introductory lab courses 6

J

Jet 21, 24, 35, 37, 41
  design 38
  motion 21
  problem handling 37
  turbine 24, 35, 41
Jet engine 33, 35, 36, 37, 38
  learning design 37
Jet principle 24, 33, 34, 35, 37, 38, 39, 41, 42, 43
  design 34
  education 37
  process 39, 42

K

Kelvin generator model 19
Kelvin's water dropper 18

L

Lab 1, 3, 4, 5, 6, 7, 8, 9
  blood pressure 6
  skills-based 4
  spectrometer 6
Lab activities 6, 7
  biomedical 7
Lab learning activities 4
Laws 2, 8, 9, 16, 17, 19, 20, 22, 35, 75, 78, 87, 88, 89
  empirical 87
  fundamental 35
  ideal gas 35
  second 89

Learning 1, 2, 3, 4, 5, 6, 9, 13, 14, 15, 16, 22, 24, 32, 33, 34, 35, 36, 37, 38, 39, 40, 41, 42, 49
  activities 2, 6, 33, 36
  dialogic 24, 49
  game-based 41
  interdisciplinary 1, 4, 9, 32
  joy of 13, 15
  procedures 42
  problem-based 16
  project-based 14, 16, 22
  strategy 33
Learning processes 2, 16, 38, 74
  effective 74
Lectures 4, 13, 17, 18, 33, 34, 35, 36, 39, 40, 66, 87, 89
  academic 87, 107
  fact-oriented 66
  introductory physics 4
  traditional 40
LED-ruler experiment 77
Lenses 5, 9, 54
Levels 14, 25, 26, 32, 33, 37, 38, 40, 55, 63, 64, 65, 66, 68, 73, 78, 79, 81, 82, 83
  atomic 73, 81
  content-oriented 55
  five interactive game 68
  interdisciplinary 14
  involving adjacent 83
  learning on a meta 40
Light 5, 6, 72, 73, 74, 75, 76, 78, 79
  chromatic structure of 75
  emission process 79
  intensity 75, 78
  matter interaction 73
Logger lite data acquisition program 96

M

Masses 33, 87, 89, 91, 92, 95, 107
  accelerated gas 33
  oscillating 87, 89, 107
Mathematical 14, 20, 102
  apparatus 14

  competence 20
  microscope 102
  statistics 20
Matrix diagonalization process 107
Measurements 5, 20, 73, 97, 98, 100, 106, 107
  acquired set of 100
  displacement 98
  involved mass 20
  spectroscopic 73
Meshchersky's equation 21
Metal comb 18
Methods 14, 15, 24, 25, 29, 72, 75, 79
  artefact 75
  didactic 24, 29
  educational 14, 15
  empirical research 72
  innovative 25
  qualitative analysis 79
Microscopic interactions 74
Model(s) 5, 14, 16, 17, 18, 19, 57, 58, 59, 60, 72, 73, 74, 77, 81, 82, 83, 84
  atomic 82
  coherent 73
  coherent quantum 73
  microscopic 83
  of educational reconstruction (MER) 72, 74, 83
  realistic quantum 77
Motion 2, 95, 96, 97, 99, 100
  oscillatory 99
  simple harmonic 5
Motion equation system 107
Motivation, cognitive 15
Municipal Sustainability Planning 65

N

Newton's laws of motion 2

O

Orbits 77, 81, 82, 83, 84
  classical 77
  physical discrete 77

Oscillations 87, 92, 100, 107
   coupled 92
   independent 92
   uncoupled 87, 92, 107
Ostensibly-relevant activities 6

P

Pedagogic foundation 49
Peer interaction 41
Phenomena 16, 17, 72, 73, 74, 75, 76, 78, 88
   capillary 17
   microscopic 73
Physical 88
   laboratory activity 88
   mathematical correlation 88
Physics 5, 19, 72, 73, 77
   apparatus, traditional 5
   modern 72, 73, 77
   of the pipe organ 19
Physics concepts 3, 4, 5, 6, 9
   applying 3
   students frame 9
Physics lab 3, 4, 6, 7, 8, 9, 25
   first didactic method 25
   introductory 3, 4, 7
Planck's hypothesis 78
Plastic wheels 96
Pre-cognitive assumptions 41
Predictions, theoretical 4
Problems 3, 14, 15, 21, 25, 38, 73, 76, 92
   complex inter-paradigmatic 25
   isomorphic 3
   structured 38
   technological 14
Procedures 38, 88
   inductive 88
   interlaced necessary 38
   sustainable 38
Processes 14, 16, 17, 19, 21, 27, 29, 34, 35, 36, 38, 42
   communicative social 35
   weaving 29
Professional 21
   foreign language competencies 21
   foreign language texts 21
   skills 21
   vocabulary 21
Projects 20, 21, 40
   developmental 40
Pulse emission system 96

Q

Quality assurance 24, 49
Quantum computers 21
Questions 9, 26, 32
   in-depth 26
   interactive 32
   open-ended 9
Quizzes 3, 26
   online 26

R

Radiation 21, 72, 73, 79, 84
   emitted 79
Reflective personality traits 20
Research 13, 14, 15, 16, 20, 22, 27, 64, 68, 72, 73, 83, 88
   activities 13, 14, 15
   competence 20
   physics education 72
   skills 13, 14, 15, 16, 22
   topic 83
   work, scientific 13
Respiratory systems 2
Revolutionised air traffic 37
Rhythmised process design 25
Rydberg's formula 76

S

Scaffolding, technology-based 40
Science 8, 9, 13, 15, 22, 26, 28, 42
   economic 26, 28
   experimental 8
   natural 22, 26, 28

Scientific students conference 21
Second didactic method 33
Self-responsible citizens 24
Sen's capability approach 41
Sensor 78, 96, 97
  digital 78
  ultrasonic 96, 97
SGC 49, 55, 56, 57, 58, 59, 60, 61, 62, 66
  level 55, 56, 57, 58, 59, 60, 61, 62
  processes 66
  rules 49
Single slit diffraction 78
Skills 3, 8, 9, 13, 14, 15, 16, 17, 20, 21, 38, 54, 65
  experimental 13, 15
  public speech 21
  scientific 9
  self-education 14
  social 65
Smoothing learning processes 35
Snell's law 9
Social 32, 39, 53, 54, 68
  and cultural geography 39
  dynamics 32, 68
  equilibriums 54
  procedures in SGC 53
Socio-ecologic competencies 65
Spectroscopy 72
Spectrum 73, 76, 77, 79, 80, 81, 82
  discrete 79, 82
  hydrogen 76
Standing waves 19
STEAM 16
  model of education 16
  program 16
Stroke engine 37
Structure 26, 29, 31, 32, 35, 36, 38, 49, 66, 72, 76, 77, 78, 79, 82
  5-level rule 49
  atomic 72
  geometric 35
  logical chain 32
  tightness of 35, 36
Student learning activities 3
Students' 13, 15, 16, 17, 68
  enthusiasm for learning 13, 15
  motivation 68
  project activities 16
  research work 13
Surface tension forces 17
Surfing global change (SGC) 34, 35, 49, 50, 51, 52, 53, 55, 64, 65, 66, 67, 68
Sustainable regimes 38
System 42, 65, 87, 89, 107
  analysis 65
  dynamics 87, 107
  global 42
  physical 87, 89, 107
  theory & biology 65

T

Teaching 7, 8, 15, 31, 32, 42, 64, 87
  assistants (TAs) 7, 8
  endeavour 87
  method 31, 32, 42, 64
  physics 15
Technologies 14, 21, 41
  advanced 14
  computer 21
Technology 14, 17
  interactive learning 17
  modern 14
Technology assessment 65
  and climate change 65
Theory 5, 8, 9, 20, 21, 73, 87, 88, 89, 101, 107
  classical gravitation 21
  joint employment of 88, 89
  modern quantum 73
  probability 20
  scientific 88
Thermal agitation 80
Time-frequency 102, 104, 105
  information 102
  plane 102, 104, 105
Topics 2, 3, 7, 8, 16, 17, 19, 20, 21, 27, 31, 32, 73, 74
  predetermined 27
Traditional 3, 37

approaches 3
education 37
Transdisciplinary 24, 27, 31, 49, 65
   action and assessment competence 31
   competence 65
Transfer, mechanical 18
Transformation, energetic 74

U

Ultrasound pulses 96

V

Virtual image 77
Visual impressions 33, 43

W

Wallerstein's world-systems theory 41
Water 18, 19
  non-distilled 19
  salted 19
  tap 19
Wavelet 87, 89, 101, 102, 104, 105, 106, 107, 108
  analysis 101, 102
  energy 106
  field 106
  transform (WT) 87, 89, 101, 102, 105, 106, 107, 108
Web 33, 40, 43, 66
  design 33, 43, 66
  platform usage 40
Web-based 40, 42, 65
  discussion 42
  quiz 65
  student activities 40
Web platform 27, 29, 31, 40, 41, 66
  dialogue-oriented 40
WT scalogram 106, 107

www.ingramcontent.com/pod-product-compliance
Lightning Source LLC
Chambersburg PA
CBHW041123300426

44113CB00002B/42